Parenting

Questions Women Ask

Parenting
Questions
Women Ask

Gail MacDonald

Karen Mains

Kathy Peel

Christianity Today, Inc.

in conjunction with

MULTNOMAH
Portland, Oregon

Cover design by Bruce De Roos

PARENTING: QUESTIONS WOMEN ASK
© 1992 by *Christianity Today, Inc.*
Published by Multnomah Press
10209 SE Division Street
Portland, Oregon 97266

Multnomah Press is a ministry of
Multnomah School of the Bible
8435 NE Glisan Street
Portland, Oregon 97220

Printed in the United States of America.

Library of Congress Cataloging-in-Publication Data

MacDonald, Gail.
    Parenting—questions women ask / Gail MacDonald, Karen Mains, Kathy Peel.
        p.   cm.—(TCW)
    ISBN 0-88070-461-6
    1. Child rearing. 2. Child rearing—Religious aspects—Christianity.
3. Parenting. I. Mains, Karen Burton. II. Peel, Kathy, 1951-   . III. Title.
IV. Series.
HQ769.M16   1992
649'.1—dc20   91-41258
                                                                                CIP

92 93 94 95 96 97 98 99 00 01 - 10 9 8 7 6 5 4 3 2 1

CONTENTS

SECTION THREE
Building Your Parenting Skills

Introduction

BEYOND PARENTING 101

A s Christian parents we are called to do one thing: "to raise our children in the nurture and admonition of the Lord." And part and parcel of this divine expectation is helping our children understand who they are in God's economy—unique boys and girls individually gifted to build his Kingdom.

Yet inherent in the task of Christian parenting are multiple challenges. How do we make the Christian faith appealing? How do we plant the seeds of self-confidence? Or how do we help our children develop a Christian sexual morality in a decaying world? It is these challenges that form the basis of this book. The answers to the questions presented in each chapter are ground in biblical principles and immensely practical.

It is our hope upon reading this book, you'll be better equipped to make God's plans for parenting a daily reality. In writing this book we sought the advice of three women whose expertise in the field of parenting comes from being on the front-lines. Gail MacDonald, Karen Mains, and Kathy Peel are not merely observers on what it's like to parent today, but rather caring, compassionate women who have changed diapers, kissed scraped knees, and listened to teenage woes. Each woman was raised in a solid Christian home and knows that the best—and most hopeful—way to effectively meet the challenges of parenting today must begin with a Christian perspective.

The chapters in this book are based on a forum conducted in Chicago in October 1990, as well as personal telephone interviews. These woman candidly shared what worked for them as well as what backfired as they ventured down the sometimes bumpy road of parenting. In addition to their insights, supplementing the discussion of these parenting concerns are excerpts from the pages of *Today's Christian Woman* magazine, as well as a section entitled, "Make It Happen," offering practical ways you can quickly and easily implement the specific suggestions made in each chapter.

About the Contributors

Gail MacDonald lives in Manhattan with her husband, Gordon, who pastors Trinity Baptist Church. Many of their experiences as parents are chronicled in the book *There's No Place Like Home* (Tyndale). Their son and daughter are both married.

"I'm a fairly structured person and so is my approach to parenting," explains Gail. "Because I have a husband who is very unstructured, we are a good compliment to each other. I think the strengths of our home have been things like listening and keeping short accounts—communicating."

Gail has extensively studied personality types, specifically the Meyers-Briggs profile. In classes at her church and in speaking engagements across the country, she explains how understanding the differences in our temperaments can help us get along with one another better. She applies this knowledge effectively throughout this book. In addition, being in a metropolitan environment and active in the many outreach programs at her church, Gail has been on the cutting edge, encountering women who face a variety of parenting challenges such as single motherhood and blended families.

Karen Mains is the mother of four children with her two youngest in college. She and her husband, David, currently live in a western suburb of Chicago and co-host a six-day-a-week radio program, *Chapel of the Air*. Karen is the author of numerous books including *Living, Loving, and Leading* (Multnomah Press), which offers insights on creating a home that encourages spiritual growth.

Karen's parenting style is best described as spontaneous and flexible—an approach that has worked well for her as she has juggled the demands of a career and family. "I'm not a disciplinarian—someone who sets up a lot of rules for my kids to keep and me to constantly enforce," admits Karen. "I think rules are fine, but we instead made our priority as parents flexibility, and this allowed us to go with the flow more often."

Listening and the ability to key in on her children's feelings and thoughts are what Karen considers her strengths as a mother. Throughout this book her "listen first, then be open" approach to solving parenting problems permeates her advice. In addition, the Mainses have worked hard to make Christian principles an appealing, natural part of their lives and are now seeing their adult children holding to the same principles.

———

Kathy Peel lives with her husband, Bill, and their three sons in Tyler, Texas. She is still in the process of raising her children, with two teenagers and a first-grader at home.

"I'm blessed to have good relationships with my children," says Kathy. "The oldest, John, teases me without mercy about his life as the first-born. He remembers being the only child who wore polished saddle shoes in the sandbox. With my third child, I'm lucky if his shoes even match.

"But there are times when John has put his arm around my shoulder and said, 'Mom, you can't cook very well, and you don't know how to sew very well, and you don't keep a very clean house, but at least we have a good time.' "

Kathy puts her fun spirit to work as president of Creative Alternatives, a firm committed to providing creative resources to strengthen busy families. Out of this background she co-wrote a best-selling series of idea books which includes *A Mother's Manual for Summer Survival* (Focus on the Family Publishing). She is also a regular contributor to *Family Circle* magazine. Her fun and practicality show up throughout the chapters to follow.

— ❧ —

As you read through the pages of *Parenting: Questions Women Ask,* we hope it helps you overcome the many hurdles you may encounter as a Christian parent with a unique commitment—to understand your children's individual, God-given personalities and gifts and then mold your children into the people God intended. But beyond that, we want this book to help you discover the immeasurable joys God has planned for you when he entrusted children to your care.

Rebecca K. Grosenbach and Marian V. Liautaud, editors

BUILDING YOUR CHILD'S CONFIDENCE AND CHARACTER

T he greatest gifts we can ever hope to give our children can't be bought—like self-confidence and an unswerving knowledge that they are loved and valued by you and God. But such confidences don't happen overnight. As Karen Mains says, it's a process that begins shortly after birth, with actions as simple as a mother's gentle stroke and loving kisses.

As our children grow and move beyond the shelter of our homes, they'll need more than confidence. They'll need a sense of character that can withstand the increasing pressures of a society whose moral base is eroding. It's this character that will help them say "no" to a world loaded with temptations and "yes" to those opportunities that will keep them on line with God's plan for their lives.

In the following chapters Gail, Karen, and Kathy offer their proven advice on nurturing independence, self-esteem, and confidence—the building blocks of your child's future.

Chapter 1

HOW CAN I NURTURE INDEPENDENCE IN MY CHILD?

Karen Mains

From the beginning, I saw my primary role as a mother as helping my children become independent of me. With each step my children took toward independence, I stood by their side saying, "Hurrah, hurrah." The first day of school, the first time they slept over at a friend's house, those were steps of independence.

For most children independence means gaining control. When a child starts to argue over what clothes he will wear or what he will eat for breakfast, it's his way of saying, "I want to decide for myself." As children reach grade school and high school, they want to choose how to spend their social time, who their friends will be, and what kinds of activities they will be involved in.

Preschoolers especially struggle to break free from the dependence they have on their parents, but at the same time, they need—and want—us to set limits for them. We can start to help our young children learn to make choices for themselves by giving them limited options. For instance, if you and your child are constantly having arguments over which cereal he will eat for breakfast, let him choose between two kinds. Be sure to let him realize the outcome of his choice by making him eat the one he has chosen. If you let him change his mind after you've poured the cereal in a bowl for him, he will be no closer to understanding how to make decisions freely and live with the consequences.

Granting Freedom to Fail

As children grow and reach the young adult stage, they exhibit their ability to be independent of us when they accept the consequences of their actions and are able to shape their existence apart from us. The struggle for us as parents is learning how to recognize their ability to make their own decisions, and then granting them the freedom to succeed—or fail.

When I was deciding whether or not one of our children should do something, I would say to the child, "Let's talk it through and see what the consequences are. Let's make sure we don't miss anything."

When my children were young, I'd use this approach over simple things, like letting them decide whether they wanted to save their dessert for after dinner or eat it after lunch instead.

As my children grew and were learning to make more significant decisions, we would think them through the options by forming questions they needed to ask of themselves. For instance, we would often ask our kids, "What do you think you can handle here? Can you play soccer after school three days a week and still have time to study? Can you handle permission to go to a certain party where there's drinking? What sort of regulations do you think you need?"

And then, we heard them out. We listened to their reasoning. I believe it is important for parents to allow their children to express themselves because, essentially, when we do, we're saying to our child, "We trust you to establish your own life."

———

Independence needs to be given in increments. For instance, we would leave a sixteen year old in charge of the house and younger siblings and go away for a day, just so that child would have an opportunity to function as the adult in the home. We tried to assess where our children's level of ability was and then give them the gift of trying something without interfering. Allowing them this freedom helped them prove their decision-making skills.

One Giant Leap

After a child successfully completes small steps of independence, he is ready to take a giant leap.

When our son, Jeremy, was fifteen, he had a passion for Japan—its culture and language. He had done some language study on his own and later we got him a tutor. He did endless amounts of research and read countless books on Japan.

Then we met a woman at a conference center who had worked in Japan, and Jeremy told her about his interest in the country. She approached me with an idea: "There's a Japanese pastor I work with. Would you like me to contact him and see if Jeremy could visit?"

So at fifteen, Jeremy was presented with the opportunity to spend the summer in Japan. I thought, *This means I would have to put him on an airplane to go to Tokyo by himself, and he would be met by a person who only speaks Japanese. . . .* Yet I could see this was a wonderful opportunity. He would be immersed in Japanese culture, living

Setting Limits

Every year we give our children more freedoms. But invariably, something will come up and make us realize, "Oh, we haven't covered that yet." When one of our sons was in kindergarten, he came home from a friend's house and said, "You won't believe the cool movie I just saw." It was a movie with violence and occult themes—something we would never watch in our own home. We needed to sit down with him and explain that while he had been given the freedom to go to his friend's house by himself, he was not old enough to watch movies there without asking us first. We didn't want him to think we were taking away his freedom, but at the same time, he needed to know what his limitations were. The whole issue of granting independence is a give-and-take process. We're learning right along with our kids.

—Kathy

15

in a non-English speaking home, and experiencing a growing Japanese church.

A Tulip or a Tree?

We used a word picture to help our children express how much independence they wanted in certain situations. We would ask, "Are you a tulip today or an oak tree?" Parents have been given as fences around fragile tulips. But an oak tree doesn't need a fence. On days the children felt weak or vulnerable, we would be their fence. On days they felt confident and strong, we would stand back.

For example, Kristen was trying to decide whether she should go to a Christian school or a public school. She had friends pulling her in both directions. She thought she could make the decision, so we said, "Good. Go ahead."

When my husband and I observed that Kristen felt inadequate in making the decision, we asked her if she felt like a tulip or an oak tree when it came to making this decision. This kept her from having to say, "I can't make this decision." She quickly said, "A tulip."

Years later, as she walked down the aisle to be married, her daddy was feeling like a tulip. Now she was feeling strong and said, "Daddy, I'll be your fence."

—Gail

As I was mulling over the decision, a friend advised me to let my son go. We had a friend for dinner one evening who happened to have been raised in Japan and she said, "If you make him wait until he's older, the inclination may not be there. You may interfere with what God is doing in this child's heart."

We heard that again from several sources. So we prayed earnestly and made our decision—we let him go. We did so because we felt the Lord had led us to it.

It was a turning point for Jeremy in every way. He came home a changed child. He was more mature, easier to live with, intrigued by other cultures. Plus he had taken spiritual leaps! It was exactly the right thing for him to do.

Another Perspective

As children become more independent and discover who they are as individuals, it's important they be affirmed by adults other than their parents. Often these adults can help children see where their strengths are and give them confidence to make their own decisions.

For instance, perhaps your teenager is trying to select a

college, but he's having a hard time deciding if he wants to live at home and commute to school, or go out of state. Sometimes an adult outsider's perspective will help your child sort through the decision-making process based on the area of interest he has seen your child excel in.

Some children become close to a school teacher or a youth leader easily. But sometimes we may have to help a child develop close ties with other adults in order for this kind of positive relationship to develop. When children form relationships with other adults, it also gives us a chance to get feedback from someone else on how our child handles freedom and makes decisions. Likewise, involving yourself in your children's world is one of the best ways to see how they are maturing.

— ≈◈≈ —

If you're involved in your children's worlds you can see what kind of people they are outside of home. That will help you determine if they're becoming trustworthy people and ready to take on more responsibility. You have to monitor the peer group influence early to know if your children use their independence wisely.

The more the sense of belonging, worth, and competence are nurtured at home, the less our children will need to find it within the peer group. One couple I know believes that if their home is a center of activity for their children's friends, they will avoid "them and us" thinking. They can observe the interactions on their porch basketball court or around the dinner table. If they see attitudes that either concern or delight them, they very naturally can bring them up later during a table conversation.

— ≈◈≈ —

Sometimes you don't know you've given a child too much freedom until he blows it. When a child does make a mistake, don't respond with blame or shame. Instead, ask, "What can we learn from this?" It's important to show sympathetic understanding, to treat our children the same way God treats us when we mess up. The reality is we learn by failure. There are stops and starts in life. By being given permission to fail and learn from our mistakes, we gain the experience to make the more important decisions that come later in life.

A Healthy Dependence

Along with helping my children become independent of me, I wanted them to become dependent upon their heavenly Father. When I began to see my children do that, I felt I had been a successful parent.

One way I tried to set them on this course was to say, "Well, let's go and ask the Lord," or "Have you prayed about that? What does the Lord say?" I didn't have to be the final authority.

I think that's where a lot of Christian parents stumble. They set themselves up as "the last word." There were times when I'd think one way about a situation and, after we'd pray, my mind would be changed. The children saw that and learned God was the final authority.

We also tried to teach our children that sometimes we make choices and then God redirects us. When he opens a door, we walk through it. But if a door is shut, we shouldn't try to force it open again because, very likely, he is trying to lead us in a different direction. I've tried to help my children learn to be accepting and grateful for the times God has intervened and shut opportunities off from them.

As parents it's scary to let our children go, to give them the freedom to make their own choices. Thankfully, we have a higher court of appeal where we can bring our concerns about our children and their ability to make independent decisions. And perhaps, when we let our children see us relying on God's wisdom rather than our own, we paint the best picture of adulthood: independent of parents and dependent upon God.

Bolstering Your Child's Confidence
Karen Dockrey

Confident children have the resources to live their faith, to resist temptation, to solve their problems, and to succeed God's way. How can we build confidence and encourage independence in our children?

• Notice and affirm when they do well: "Your words showed understanding. I'm proud of the way you cared for your friend."

• Find strengths related to every weakness: "You ran hard after that soccer ball!" rather than "Why can't you learn how to kick the ball properly!"

• Downplay criticism. When you have to criticize, focus on the action rather than the child: "Being late makes it hard to trust you," rather than "You're always late! I'll never be able to trust you again."

• Point out something positive about frustrations: "Even though you were late, you did call. That shows consideration and a sense of responsibility."

• Help children solve their own problems: "How might we master this lateness problem? I know it's as frustrating for you as it is for me." Together with your child, list several possibilities and implement one.

• Guide your children to evaluate their actions. Ask: "What went well in your plan?" "What might we have done even better?" "What actions would you change if you could do it again?"

• Accept thoughts and feelings: "I'd be disappointed

too," rather than "Those things happen; don't let it get you down." Accepting what your children say and feel encourages them to trust their insights and discover what God wants them to do next.

• Allow your children to make their own choices. The best way to gain confidence in making right choices is to practice: Offer your toddler the choice between two outfits. Teach your third grader how to look at the thermometer and decide how warmly to dress.

• Cultivate listening times that can be counted on, rather than depending on spontaneous opportunities: At supper, encourage family members to share the best and worst event of their day. Invite your children to help with a daily task during which you can talk.

• Let your children know you need them: "I don't know what we'd do without your gift ideas at birthday time! You always know just what to buy Jessica!"

• Be a guinea pig. Receiving your children's compliments with enthusiasm encourages them to develop their own affirmation skills: "Thank you. Your words make me feel wonderful!"

From Today's Christian Woman
(May/June 1988)

Make It Happen

1. If your children are young, think through the kind of independence you would like them to have when they reach high school. Outline the steps it will take to get them there so you can give them certain responsibilities as they grow up.

2. Learn to "debrief" your child after he makes a mistake in judgment. Find out the reasons he decided the way he did, the consequences of his decision, what he may need to do to "repair the damage," and what he has learned that he can apply to the future. This will seem awkward at first, but after a few times your child will begin to process these questions himself.

3. When your children make mistakes, recall times you made mistakes and share those experiences with them. Relating how a failure proved a turning point in your life will bring perspective to your children's disappointment.

Chapter 2

HOW CAN I MOTIVATE MY CHILD?

Gail MacDonald

H elping our children develop their skills to the fullest is a critical responsibility we parents hold. Yet, as a mother, I also have learned that this can be one of the most frustrating tasks. There's nothing worse than watching a child squander talent or fail to live up to his potential. In my effort to motivate my children to be all they can be, I've come to realize that there are some basics that need to be established before we can hope to light a fire under our kids.

We need to determine our primary purpose for parenting. As I was raising our children, I realized that the ultimate goal for me as a parent was to see my children come to know and obey the Lord. Keeping this goal in mind helped me stay focused on my primary objective of developing their sense of spirituality. In turn, I spent less time worrying about whether they were making top grades in every class or excelling in sports. So the first step we can take toward effectively motivating our children is to determine exactly where we want to see them grow.

—⋘⋙—

I believe God gave us the model for helping our children realize their full potential in the way he responded to his Son.

23

When Jesus began his earthly ministry, God gave him three things all of us long for. First, a sense of acceptance when he said, "This is my beloved Son," and second, a sense of worth, "in whom I am well pleased (Matthew 3:17, KJV). Later he added competence when he said, "Listen to him" (Mark 9:7). If we successfully bless our children with these same gifts, I am convinced they will be much more self-motivated.

How do children feel accepted? Through touch, initially. We can see how key this is even in the very first hours of a child's life. A newborn will quickly take to breast-feeding with all of its warmth and closeness. Both eye contact and body contact help offer the security that was so important in the womb.

Later they feel they belong when we maintain certain routines that give them a sense of security and well-being. Children also gain acceptance by feeling they are an integral part of the family.

By imparting a sense of worth—not for what our children do or how they look, but for who they are—we let them know that they are special in every way. We reinforce the fact that their bodies are wonderful, their minds are amazing, and their emotions are a gift from God.

Children also need a sense of competence. They're motivated to do what they naturally do best, so as Karen said in the preceding chapter, we need to look for their abilities and strengths and praise them for those.

We tried to motivate our children largely through praise, rarely through criticism (except during the "terrible twos"). And we made it a point to congratulate each child for every success along the way. You don't have to wait until the child is totally competent or until he does something exactly right. Praise any sign of progress.

Beyond the Basics

Howard Hendricks taught years ago that relationship always precedes rule—and it's a principle that applies when we're trying to build new skills into our children's lives. Children will accept our rules if they first accept us. Where there is no relationship, children will defy and rebel against their parents. So we always have to concentrate on the relationship first, make sure we're communicating, make sure that our children feel they belong, are worthwhile, and competent. Once we're sure we're meeting these basic needs in a fairly consistent manner, and we have in mind the larger goals we want to accomplish in their lives, we're ready to concentrate on some of the specifics of effective motivation.

The first rule of thumb I learned was to motivate by describing tasks so the child knew when he had completed it correctly. Then I gave either affirmation or correction.

When our children were small and they didn't do their chores, Gordon and I found it all too easy to become nags. So we set a clock, and if the clock went off and the chores were not done, the children had to pay the consequences. That way the clock was the culprit.

Putting the Pieces Together

I think where we often err as parents is in trying to motivate all of our children the same way. While it's effective to motivate one child by giving rewards, another child will respond better to praise. It pays to study each child to learn what motivates them most effectively.

—Kathy

Whenever possible, link the consequences with the action. One of our children didn't like to keep his room clean. So one day I didn't wash clothes, and I said, "I thought we'd make a little deal here. You clean your room, Mom cleans the clothes. We need each other." And the point was made.

Getting a child to cooperate in the family out of love will be easier if they see the purpose of certain chores. I remember how I failed to do this with our son. One day he said to me, "I hope I never have to vacuum again. I'm sick of vacuuming! It's a stupid job. Why do I have to do it?" It had been a long time since I had explained to him the reason I needed him to help me. I apologized to him and told him that by vacuuming he was helping me and therefore showing he loved me, just as by washing his clothes I was helping him and showing him love. I pointed out that every family requires cooperation, that we couldn't make it without each other. That gave him a whole new perspective on vacuuming.

It's right to try to motivate our children to be more responsible, but we must do it out of love and in a way that is effective for each particular child. A friend of mine has a son who's responsible for mowing the lawn. The son doesn't enjoy this job, but he does care about what other people think of him. His parents know this, so they motivate him by pointing out what a good job he does. They tell him everyone in the neighborhood says, "That boy really does a good job keeping their lawn looking good."

Welcome to My World

If a mother doesn't show she cares about her children's world, it's unlikely the children will care about her world. So if you want your children to respond to the chore side of life, you've got to make time for the things that are important to them, too.

—*Karen*

We have to motivate children in ways in which they "hear" they are competent. But we also need to know when to back-off. Our daughter had little interest in learning how to cook. I decided to wait until the need arose in her instead of forcing her to learn to like to cook. It was only when she was about to get married and looked forward to being a homemaker that she said, "Mom, teach me to cook."

Part of Their World

Another key factor in motivating our children to be their most competent and best selves is to spend time being in their world. One day a local radio station producer wanted me to come in to tape an interview. I said I couldn't; I had to be at our son's soccer game that day. The man said, "I know you and Gordon like to have someone cover for your son's games, so maybe Gordon could cover for you." By his tone I realized that the man thought I was attending the game merely out of a sense of duty, that the parental thing to do was go to soccer games.

But he was so wrong. Gordon and I loved going to the games. We didn't want to miss them. It was one way of being in our son's world, which gave us a chance to praise him for his performance and team spirit.

No matter how we're trying to motivate our children, the manner in which we do it is key. I once heard a story about a woman who tried to force cod liver down her dog's throat. It was always an ordeal. She would hold his head, pry his mouth open, and shoot it down his throat. One day, she dropped the bottle, and, in scrambling to get it before the cod liver oil ran out of it, she let go of the dog's mouth. The next thing she knew the dog was lapping up the cod liver oil from the floor. It wasn't that he didn't like the oil; he didn't like the way she fed it to him.

Over time I've come to realize that whether I'm motivating my children in large areas or small, the key is how I'm going about doing it. Almost without fail, when I have encouraged them out of love, affirming their worth, and providing opportunities for them to grow in their competence, they have surpassed my hopes in striving to realize their unique potential.

Make It Happen

1. Experiment with different motivation techniques until you find one that works for each child. Try rewards and incentives, try public praise, try reinforcing the sense of accomplishment. Keep in mind your children's response to each method as you search for effective ways to motivate them.

2. Pay attention to the kinds of chores your children complain most about. Maybe you could swap responsibilities or rotate jobs between the children so they aren't always called upon to do those things they dislike.

3. Remember that children are imitators. The attitude with which you go about your daily tasks will rub off on your children.

Chapter 3

CAN I KEEP
MY CHILD FROM BEING
SELF-CENTERED?
Gail MacDonald

When our children were young, they learned a little song to sing whenever they were being selfish with their toys. "A sharing time is a happy time, a happy time, a happy time. We share our toys and we share our books, and that's a happy time." To this day, our married daugther and I still sing that song whenever we feel one of us is being selfish. It lightens the moment with a bit of humor, but at the same time it calls attention to the persistent problem of selfishness we all face—not just children.

Before we can hope to develop a giving spirit in our children, we need to first confront our own selfishness and concentrate on displaying true generosity for our children.

In our home, it was very important for me to admit my own selfishness and to identify with our children when they were feeling selfish. I would say to them very directly, "You know, Mommy feels selfish sometimes, too. The other day I felt selfish, and this is what I did. . . ." Then I would ask our children to pray for me. It's important for them to understand that Mom

29

and Dad still fight these feelings as well. It isn't just a child's problem.

It also helped our children understand selfishness was more than a bad habit, it was sin. And to do this I used stories from Scripture and from real life. This gives us a way to flush out the negative effects of selfishness as well as the positive consequences of generosity.

Selfish By Whose Standards?

As you are thinking about how to train your children in unselfish behaviors, be sure you are not imposing your definition of selfishness on your child according to your own personality. For instance, an outgoing mother who enjoys being surrounded by people may think that her child who enjoys playing alone is being selfish, when that is not the case at all.

—Kathy

Perhaps the most graphic account of the consequences of selfishness is the story of Ananias and Sapphira (Acts 5:1-11). From a positive point of view, Jesus himself said it is more blessed to give than to receive (Acts 20:35). And Paul praises generosity all through his letters to young churches. He gives a specific example in 2 Corinthians 8:2-3: "Out of the most severe trial, their overflowing joy and their extreme poverty welled up in rich generosity. For I testify that they gave as much as they were able, and even beyond their ability."

Nurturing a Generous Spirit

One of the biggest challenges in developing a child's generous spirit is to instill proper motives for sharing and giving. Bible stories help us teach proper motives, but beyond that we need to rely on prayer. As we strive to model generosity for our kids, we can pray that our words and actions reflect the generous Christ so much so that our children are drawn to act like him. The more our own thoughts are focused on Jesus and his actions, the more a true spirit of generosity will develop in us, and our children will sense the authenticity of our actions.

We also can pray that our children will feel God's pleasure most when they are giving to others. You might come up with a strategy in your family for being generous to your neighbors. Maybe there's a new mom on the block who would love a home-cooked meal. Perhaps there's an elderly widow who needs companionship. There might be a single parent who could be invited over for dinner.

Often, children think of wonderfully creative ways to meet these needs. When they do, let them do the giving, and let them see the joy on a neighbor's face. This way, your children will learn that giving is the best way to live because of the response it generates and the good feelings they experience. You won't need to convince them with words.

As we pray for them and model unselfish giving based on proper motives, the maturing work of Christ in their lives will strengthen them and build in them an authentic spirit of giving.

———❧———

For some children, giving will come more naturally. However, some children are inclined to give materially, while others may give of themselves— their thoughts, their songs, and so on. We need to be attentive to the many ways our children display generosity and be careful not to undermine their efforts. Be sure to praise them whenever you see them giving of themselves, realizing that for one child giving may mean sharing his toys; for another, it may mean listening to a friend who's having a hard time at home. However generosity is displayed, we need to let our kids know that we appreciate their efforts and Jesus is happy to see them sharing.

Give in Proportion

When my children became young adults, they started telling my husband and me that their needs were not being met. They felt we were giving too much of our time, attention, resources, and energy to other people. What I learned from them was that we need to develop a healthy sense of giving. It's okay to establish boundaries in giving, to say, "I can do this for you, but I cannot do this." If you raise children without a sense of proportion in giving, they are vulnerable, as we were, to feeling they have to serve every needy person they come into contact with. It's possible to over-give, and in doing so lose the joy of giving and doing for others.

—Karen

Make It Happen

1. Cultivating a giving spirit starts at home. Model unselfish behavior toward your spouse, your own friends, your kids, and their friends as well. Show your children the joy of doing nice things for their siblings, for Dad—and Mom. Do special things for them so they can remember how good it made them feel and inspire them to do the same for someone else.

2. Make giving and sharing a natural part of family life. When you bake cookies, think of someone to share them with. When you plan a holiday meal, think of someone special to invite. Ask your children for ideas. For example, if there is a sick child in the neighborhood, ask your children what they could do to make their friend feel better. Guide your children until they come up with an idea you can carry out. And remember, not all ideas will be "things." There's nothing better than prayer!

3. Pray specifically and aloud with your children, planting positive thoughts and behaviors into their minds. You might say, "Thank you, God, that James is such a nice boy and that he shares his toys," even on a day when your son has been extremely selfish. Trust that it is God's will for him to be kind and unselfish.

4. Orchestrate teaching opportunities where you can observe their behavior, and then talk about it later when you are alone. For example, you can invite some of your children's class members to your home for a party or activity, and see firsthand how your children treat their peers. Later you can talk about what you saw, praising them for the positive ways they acted toward their friends, and lovingly guiding them toward more positive behavior in the future.

5. Look for children's books that demonstrate selflessness. These will help your child understand the importance of sharing.

Chapter 4

HOW CAN I NURTURE MY CHILD'S SELF-ESTEEM?
Karen Mains

One of the greatest gifts we can bestow on our children is a healthy sense of self-esteem—a confidence in themselves and the knowledge that they are valued. Children who grow up without realizing their value inevitably spend the rest of their lives trying to win the approval they never received at home.

While we might not realize it, a child's self-image begins forming shortly after birth. The child's initial self-concept is found in his mother's face—the delight in her eyes, the sound of her voice—it's a mirroring effect. The way she holds him, the cooing, the baby language, all have a significant impact on the child's developing self-image.

Expressing delight in our children often comes most naturally when they are young. What mother hasn't applauded her child's first attempt to walk or say "Mommy"? But as children grow older, we need to continue to delight in them and show respect for the way God made them. And it is through our showing this respect that they come to respect themselves. We need to constantly affirm the things we see in them that are wonderful and encourage them to develop the positive qualities they possess.

- ❧ -

I operate under the theory that within each child is a clue of what he has been made to be. One of the greatest ways to show a child we respect him is to do as much as we can to follow these clues.

Another Day, Another Try

In John 17, Jesus says to the Father, "They have kept thy word." Talk about putting the crown four inches over their head and saying, "Grow into it!" The disciples were doing anything but keeping the word. In fact, they were arguing over who was going to be the greatest among them. And yet Jesus as much as says, "You may not be doing it today, but I have great hope for you tomorrow." I think this is one of the key ways we build self-esteem in our children. If our parenting says, "Even though you might have failed today, tomorrow you're going to get it right," then our children gain a sense that we believe in them and all they can be.

—Gail

My husband and I encouraged any interest our children displayed, within reason financially. We let them pursue their passions as far as they were interested, with only a little bit of parental encouragement along the way. If a fledgling whim didn't take hold, I just assumed their particular genius was in another area. A parent affirms and respects a child's struggle to discover what God has planted within him. We need to clearly communicate that we believe in our children and that we're ready to aid them in that self-discovery.

For instance, Joel, our third child, went through clarinet, piano, guitar, gymnastics, and puppetry, yet never mastered anything. We eventually found out his real skill is in producing—overseeing many components.

Randall, our oldest, was the collector—he had thousands of stamps and aluminum cans, which ended up in our attic. What I came to understand during those grade school years is that he's an architect of systems. Now, as an adult, he's in charge of finances and operations at the Chapel of the Air, and he does a fine job organizing everything efficiently and creatively.

Melissa, our only daughter, was exceedingly shy as a child, yet very dramatic at home. I wanted to help her feel comfortable in outside situations, so I joined a mime troupe with her. Years later she ended up majoring in theater in college.

Another way to search out clues to our children's strengths and to show you respect them is to take time to listen. I always made it a point to grant each child their own talking time. For one that meant spending time listening to the details of his day right after he got home from school. For the others, it would be at nighttime after I had gotten ready for bed. They'd gather in my bedroom to chat about the day. The fact that I took the time to listen and to discover when each of them felt most comfortable talking gave them a sense of being valued.

Words Will Hurt Me

While there are plenty of ways to develop our children's self-esteem, too often we fall into patterns that achieve the exact opposite. Mean, cutting, or harsh words—even words that are meant in jest—can do lasting damage to our children's self-image. We need to carefully consider our choice of words with our kids. Like their peers who call them names and ridicule them, we can easily belittle our children by teasing them. In anger, too, we may say things to our children that we don't mean, but often our words leave an indelible mark on the way they view themselves. We must take care never to call our children names. If you make a mistake, be quick to apologize. Don't allow your children to carry self-reproach with them through life.

As parents, so much of our ability to nurture our children's self-esteem is related to how positive our own self-image is. For instance, if you feel you're unattractive or unintelligent, you

Shifting the Focus

Being interested in your children's world is critical for developing their self-esteem. When our son John ran for president of student council and lost, he was very disappointed. We took him out for dinner and built him up by telling him why we thought he was a wonderful person. You can help a disappointed child by taking his focus off his disappointment and putting it onto something he feels good about.

—Kathy

may be unwittingly projecting the same negative feelings onto your children. One way to gauge whether or not you are doing this is to listen to what you say to them. If criticism and negative comments are the only words flowing from your mouth regarding yourself, there's a good chance you need to concentrate on building your own self-image as well as your child's.

Thankfully, Christ helps us. Knowing we are made in his image, we can pass this ultimate sense of worth guaranteed by our Creator on to our children.

The Aaron Chronicles
Janet Bly

A friend's call to announce an unexpected pregnancy sparked my familiar monologue on Aaron, our "surprise baby."

"At least you don't have two almost grown sons, like we did," I told her. Then I spied four-year-old Aaron, peeking around the corner. Suddenly I recalled all the times I chattered away about my "surprise baby." For the first time, it hit me how my words might affect him. How often had my children heard words like these, words that may be translated in the private places of their hearts to mean "unwanted." I decided to wage a campaign to diminish the harmful effect of my innocent, but often insensitive words and actions.

One evening I started telling "Aaron Chronicle" stories to offset the effect of my "surprise baby" monologue. I told Aaron all about the day he was born, how his brothers named him, how his name meant "bringer of light." My husband joined in with what everyone thought and said the day we brought Aaron home and what fun he added to our family. Aaron loves these stories, especially when he has a bad day.

Chronicle stories of how God brought a child into your life can be developed for adopted children and step-children as well. Children long to know they're somewhere at the center of your attention and admiration. Where does your child shine? What do you admire most about him? Building a child's self-esteem and sense of belonging within the family does not have to be difficult, as I discovered.

From Today's Christian Woman
(September/October 1989)

Boost Your Teens' Esteem
Bonnie Bruno

How can we continue to nurture our kids when they don't want to be treated like "kids" anymore?

What frustrates many of us is that the method we use on our teens today may fall flat tomorrow. However, because adolescents can be unpredictable, we must handle them lovingly and cautiously.

Listen to their music. If you're like me, you probably get a good workout each day stomping to your teen's bedroom door to beg, "Pleee-ease turn down your stereo!"

Imagine his shock when you take the time to ask the name of his favorite musical group, whether or not they write their own lyrics, and what makes them unique.

Ask your teen for advice. It may come as a

shock to your adolescent that you actually value his input.

Teenagers, who so often feel trapped between childhood and adulthood, will jump at the chance to express their ideas. Showing you value their input and respect their opinions raises their self-esteem a notch or two.

Look for ways to compliment them. Many times our natural instinct is to correct. Our teens experience days when they thirst like a droopy, neglected ivy. A single compliment will work wonders at such moments. Proverbs 15:23 explains the results of choosing our words carefully: "A man finds joy in giving an apt reply—and how good is a timely word!"

Let them treat you. One way to encourage children to become adults is by allowing them the privilege of picking up the tab when they offer to.

Maybe it's a steaming cup of coffee at McDonald's on your way home from the grocery store, or a hot dog at the football game. Answering, "Thanks, but you better hang on to your money," is like splashing cold water in your child's face.

When we learn to accept our teen's gifts graciously—no matter how great or small—we are, in essence, returning that love.

Control your shock. Whether the topic is who's doing drugs at school or the latest rumored pregnancy, practice listening to your teen with your mouth shut. If you must speak, it's better to ask questions than sermonize.

When your teen comes to you and admits a personal mistake, how do you react? Did you ever consider the courage it takes for him to ask for forgiveness?

One of the ways God nurtures us is by granting us his undivided attention. He hears us out, regardless of what we've done. Discipline may come later, but his initial reaction is one of gentleness and compassion. Maybe that's why we feel free to approach him time and time again, knowing he'll listen and forgive.

From Today's Christian Woman
(November/December 1990)

Make It Happen

1. Begin to comment on the things your children do right, from setting the table to putting a bike away. Your praise will show you value their contributions to the family and encourage them to take pride in a job well done.

2. Ask your children what activities they have always wanted to do, but haven't yet pursued. If possible, give them opportunities to explore new interests.

3. If your self-esteem is lacking, pursue some of your own untapped talents. Finding something you excel in can be a real esteem booster you can pass along to your children.

Chapter 5

HOW CAN I APPRECIATE AND UNDERSTAND MY CHILD FOR THE UNIQUE PERSON HE IS?
Gail MacDonald

A friend of mine once admitted that her two children are so different from each other that she actually finds it difficult to "like" both of them equally. Her tendency was to favor the child who was more like her. However, one day she realized the Lord had given her just the children she needed to help conform her to the image of Christ. And to make that happen she knew she needed to understand and appreciate her children for the unique individuals they were.

A child who is unlike us in personality is often a puzzle. We might find ourselves asking, "Why is this child doing this?" Is this defiant behavior or simply a difference in personalities? Knowing the answers to these questions can remove a lot of grief and conflict.

For instance, I know a meticulous woman who has a sloppy son. After years of battling with him over messy rooms and a messy lifestyle, the woman finally admitted there was nothing morally wrong with his behavior. Sure, every child must learn some degree of self-discipline and order. But a neat person is not morally superior to a messy one. For her, once she knew her son was sloppy because he was more interested in other things, she was in a better position to help him deal with his weaknesses and capitalize on his strengths.

Learning to Love the Differences

There are four questions we need to ask ourselves to help us learn to understand and appreciate the differences in our children.

First ask, *What energizes my child?* Does he love being where the action is, playing with others? Or does he prefer spending time alone? For the more extroverted child, being with people charges him up, while the introvert is drained when he has to spend a lot of time with others.

Both of our children enjoyed people, but when they came home, they wanted to be alone. Giving my daughter, Kristy, her space and not misreading her closed door was important. Parents who barge into an introverted child's room without knocking may cause resentment. Kristy's quiet time was her time to process the day—to think things through. Because I am an extrovert, I tend to prefer doing "noisy thinking," which means I think as I talk. So it was hard for me to understand why some of my family needed so much time to do inner thinking before talking. Recognizing this without making value judgments will enable children who process within themselves that freedom.

The second question to ask yourself about your child is, *How does my child take in information?* Some children will rely on their five senses—seeing, hearing, touching, tasting and smelling—as they perceive the world and everything that happens to them in it. They're observant and pay attention to detail. But others rely more on their intuition. These children are less likely to care about details. They like to daydream and make up things.

My husband is the creative, intuitive type, and says he remembers his teachers always used to say, "Gordon, you dream too much. Quit looking out the window, and come back to reality."

He eventually wrote his first novel at age eleven, and instead of being met with affirmation for a good beginning, those around him laughed, not realizing Gordon's sensitive nature.

Intuitive types need a great deal of affirmation. They also require more patience: caring about details doesn't come naturally to them, so they may lose things easily. On the positive side, though, intuitive children can delight you with their imagination and creativity.

The third question to ask is, *How does my child make decisions?* The child who prefers *thinking* will drive you crazy with "why" questions when he is small. This child decides according to logic, facts, and principles. As a parent, if you fail to think through your responses logically, or treat your child unfairly, you will run the risk of losing your child's respect. "Thinking" children like rules in games, and if anyone breaks the rules, watch out!

Other children prefer to make decisions based on what's best for other people and themselves. These are the *feeling* types. They have a strong need for harmony in relationships, and, because they tend to take things personally, their feelings are easily hurt.

Seeing the Beauty

One of the things I had to do was pray that God would give me his love for my children. Then I allowed God to open my eyes to what was beautiful in each child. Generally, the same quality that makes a child seem obnoxious has a flip side that is a wonderful quality. Randall's strong will, for instance, carried with it the ability for intense concentration.

I prayed for divine love for my children, then I watched for God to reveal to me the children's beautiful qualities.

—Karen

The way our children make decisions gives us a clue in part to the fourth question that helps us understand our child's personality—*How does my child prefer to relate to the outside world?*

Typically, children who make decisions quickly, and who expect their parents to make decisions quickly, too, love making choices. They have strong opinions and well-thought-out goals. Such children work before they play, and tend to be organized and have orderly rooms. They thrive on schedules and plans.

To encourage children like this, you need to help them make good decisions and understand their need to schedule and plan. I know because I am this kind of person. I can remember when I was growing up, if I didn't know what the plan was the night before something was to happen, I would actually get a nervous stomach. I needed to know what was happening. The downside of this way of making decisions is that one can make a poor decision based on insufficient information, simply because one feels better having it decided.

Spreading the Love Around

Just before the birth of our second child, I remember thinking, How can I ever love another child as much as I love the first one? What I didn't understand was that you love all your children differently. They're all unique and God gives you that love for each one.

—Kathy

My husband, on the other hand, grew up feeling exactly the opposite. He prefers not to plan. He's the type who values spontaneity and is forever curious. And he doesn't like to make decisions until he feels all the information is in.

While this type of child dislikes being forced into making premature decisions, the downside is he may put things off too long and procrastinate. If a child is like this, you may be convinced he's delaying simply to be obstinate. In thinking this, though, you put a "value judgment" on something which is simply the child's preferred way of dealing with decisions. Pushing will only make matters worse. Instead, as a parent, we need to help the child gather information and then encourage him to make a decision, letting him know that we understand it's difficult to decide, but we know he'll make a good decision when it's time.

Children who value spontaneity over schedule will also fail to see value in keeping their rooms tidy. Don't take this personally, thinking your child is deliberately trying to spite you. To him, cleaning up his room is a complete waste of time. You have to decide if keeping a tidy room is something that's important to you. If it's not, then just close the door. If it is, there are gentle ways you can try to get your point across.

For instance, one of our children was the type who didn't see the point of order. The chair in this child's room was piled high with clothes, so I put a little note on the chair that said, "Did you know that chairs full of clothes become demon possessed?" And I drew a little smiley face on the note. The child came to me after reading the note and said, "Oh, Mom, you're funny. I'll clean the chair." Humor can go a long way in helping us deal with others' annoying habits and motivating them to be their best selves.

Be Slow to Label

A word of caution as you read this and consider your child's unique personality. Beware of making statements that lock a child into a type of behavior, like "You're a thinker and always will be." It may take years before you can be sure how strong your children's preferences are. Humans are a composite. Ideally, all of us will learn new ways of responding to each other that take us beyond our own preferred style of relating to the world.

Although all of us want to understand our children's behavior better, we still need to hold them accountable for being on time, keeping their rooms and belongings fairly ordered, and dealing with people. We obviously can't let them be what their natural inclination is all their lives. What we need to do is help them develop a more appropriate response if their natural preference is not adequate. Understanding temperament differences may help illuminate why you tend to favor one child over another or have a difficult time relating to a child. And, as you understand the specifics of your children's personalities, you'll be better able to appreciate the strengths and weaknesses of their "style," as well as your own. This understanding can go a long way in promoting family harmony, fostering self-esteem, and valuing your children for the unique people they are.

Make It Happen

1. Reread the story of Jacob and Esau to reinforce the dangers of preferring one child over another (Genesis 25-27).

2. Figure out the personality types of you and each of your children. Which children are like you? Who is the most unlike you? Think of the areas of conflict you encounter with your children. Do they line up with the differences in your personality types? Write down the "danger zones" between you and each of your children, and add them to your prayer list. You might also want to read the book *One of a Kind* by LaVonne Neff (Multnomah).

3. Once you know your children's personality preferences, analyze whether your parenting approach lines up with the children's needs. For instance, if you discover you have an "intuitive" child, are you giving him extra doses of affirmation?

4. Pray that God would give you the eyes of Christ toward your children, seeing them as irreplaceable, likable, and unique. The change in your home will be remarkable.

Chapter 6

HOW CAN I ENCOURAGE MY CHILD TO OPEN UP TO ME?
Kathy Peel

One day our youngest, James, asked me something, and I totally ignored him. He asked me four times and then said, "Mom, are you listening to me at all?"

Even though the question he was asking was not a life and death matter, it was important to him—important enough that I stop what I was doing and give him some focused attention. His reaction made me realize that if I want my children to be open with me, I need to cultivate an atmosphere and a relationship that will make it easy for them to communicate. It also showed me how important it is to establish good communication patterns early. One of the ways we can begin to do this is by asking ourselves, *Am I the kind of person my children would want to talk to? Am I a good listener? Do I look interested when my children are trying to tell me something?*

We also create an open atmosphere when Mom and Dad show genuine interest in each of the kids and what's happening in their lives. For instance, even though I don't like some of my kids' music, I'll ask my sons questions about it. I find out why they like a certain artist or song.

Another way I try to cultivate open communication with our kids is to protect our time together as a family. I've found that morning is our best time for sharing, so I make a big deal over having an unhurried breakfast. That means I have to get up early, but it's worth the effort. We sit down and talk about what is coming up, who has what on their schedule. This also helps prevent little surprises like finding out about a baseball practice thirty minutes before my son needs to be there.

We also encourage openness by asking specific questions. "How was your day?" will probably get a "Fine" answer. Try questions like, "What was the best thing that happened at preschool today?" or the worst thing. Instead of "How was the baseball game?" you might say, "Did anyone strike out? Did anyone get a home run? Did you feel good about what you did? Did anything funny happen?"

Keeping Your Lips Zipped

As our children begin to talk more freely, we need to listen without making judgments. The key is to "respond" instead of "react," no matter what they say. If my boys come home from school and tell me something bad they did, I try to respond calmly instead of saying, "(Gasp) I can't believe my ears. How could you do something like that?" and then give a sermon. I try to keep my lips zipped until I can speak calmly. Right after you hear something upsetting or startling, it's easy to fly off the handle and say things that will turn off your children. You need to let all your emotions settle before you can address the essential issues.

When a sermon is called for, we need to make sure our child is ready to hear. For instance, when my oldest son was sixteen, he had a huge history project due that we'd been talking about for a week. He's usually pretty good about keeping up with projects, but this time he waited until the last minute to finish. So here we were at midnight, sitting in front of the computer, trying to get this thing done. I was helping because I can type faster than he can. I wanted so badly to give him a lecture. But that wouldn't do any good. He didn't need correction right then. The time to talk would be after he gets the grade back, whether it's good or bad. By then the emotions surrounding the event would have subsided and he could reflect on the late night tension and draw his own conclusions. And by waiting to make my point, I didn't make him resentful toward me.

Tackling the Tough Issues

Even though children don't like to be preached at, there is a time to sit down and talk through some tough issues. If you hear there's a group of kids who started drinking in seventh or eighth grade, then you need to talk about it when your child is in sixth grade. Be prepared. Don't hide your head in the sand. Say, "You're going to be approached about drinking and you're going to have to decide before then how you're going to respond."

We went so far as to invite our two teenage sons out for dinner to talk about the pressures they're under and the decisions they're having to make. We told them, "Taking a stand for what is right is going to be lonely." Then we gave them a ring as a symbol, thanking them for being good kids so far. It also serves as a reminder that God is always with them to give them strength.

Open the Shade

There are moments in our children's lives when they open up a shade and say, "Here I am, look in." Often these come when children are sick, when they're going to bed, or when they're in the midst of failure or exhilaration. I call those "open window moments." As difficult as it is given our busy lifestyles, we need to make a point to be available to them, because those brief, spontaneous moments are the times when they are most likely to share who they really are with us.

—Gail

When you sit down to discuss serious issues with your children, ask questions so it becomes a two-way conversation. For instance, if the topic is drinking, find out what your children know about alcohol (the dangers of addiction and illness), if they know kids who drink, how they feel about it, and if they have any questions like, "Are wine coolers bad?" As you give them a chance to speak, they'll learn they can come to you with serious problems or questions.

Most every family has a packed schedule these days, so sometimes you have to orchestrate opportunities for children to be open with you. Once I had to go out of town on a short business trip, and I pulled my sixteen-year-old out of school a little early to drive with me just so we could have a few hours in the car to talk. I try to make specific times to be alone with each of our three boys. Often it's in the car. I'll let them play their music, as long as we can talk over it. With younger kids, you might say, "What songs did you sing in preschool today?" or "What did you learn in your swim class today?" With the teenagers I'll say, "Who's going together?" "How is your friend, Heather, doing? I know she had a hard time last semester." You don't want to be nosey, yet you want to be interested. Make positive editorial comments such as, "Well, I hate to hear that he's been experimenting with drugs. He's such a nice guy. We need to pray for him."

Have I Got a Question

We made sure the children were a part of adult conversations. When guests came over for dinner, we played a game where each child could ask two questions of the guest, and the guest had to answer the question as honestly as possible. Through that process the children became used to asking questions—one of the basic ingredients of good communication.

—Karen

Finding a Prime Time

It's important to me to be able to pick up each child myself after school because I find out a lot of information when the children get in the car. It's one-on-one time while events are still fresh on their minds. As I pick up each subsequent child, the first ones are quiet. There's a little bit of conversation bouncing back and forth between the others, but they know that as each sibling is picked up, it's my time to check in with him and find out about the day. And if something bad has happened, it'll usually come out.

If you're a working mom, you may not be able to do this. But maybe you can touch base by telephone in the afternoon, as soon as that child gets home. Let him know that, even though you're not there physically, you're thinking about him, and you care about his world. You might be able to ask, "Tell me what you did today. What can I do to help your schedule run better tonight? Is there anything I can pick up for you on the way home from work? Let me tell you where I left a snack for you."

I also take advantage of bedtime. Although I don't tell stories or sing songs to the older ones anymore, I give them a back scratch or a massage. It's nice to sit beside their bed and talk quietly. Kids tend to be more open at night when the lights are out, they're tired, and their defenses are down.

When our children open up about their feelings, we need to be careful not to discount their emotions. If they say, "I hate my music class. It's boring," and we react by saying, "Too bad, you shouldn't feel that way," that's not a good way to encourage further discussion. First, find out what they mean by "boring." Ask them to describe what goes on. It may, in fact, be boring. Or music may not be an area of interest for that child. By showing respect for their feelings, even if you eventually do address their attitude, you encourage openness and free communication.

It's Never Too Early

It pays to start practicing good communication early. When kids hit adolescence, they tend to withdraw from us and feel threatened by our attempts to get them to share their lives with us. If you haven't established good patterns for communication, don't expect to wake up one day and say, "You're sixteen, now we're going to communicate." Productive, honest communication is built over time and it's based on trust and mutual respect.

Whatever age your children are, though, it's a worthwhile investment of time and energy to begin implementing some of these communication ideas now. It may take time to feel you've reached the level of closeness you desire with your children, but the payback is worth every minute of your time.

How Do You Feel About . . . ?
Bill Peel

When our children were young, I devised this tool to help develop open communication with our children. You can tailor the questionnaire to fit your child's age level and particular issues you might be dealing with. This form is geared for nine to twelve year olds.

————◆————

We would like to have your honest answers to these questions. Please tell us how you really feel, not what you think we want to hear.

How Important Do You Feel?

Write a plus sign if you feel more important than what is listed, a minus sign if you feel less important, and an equal sign if you feel as important as what is listed.

TO MY DAD, I feel more (+) less (-), or equally (=) important than:
___ his work
___ his tools
___ his friends
___ his rest/recreation
___ his car
___ his relationship with Mom
___ his relationship to God
___ his yard
___ the church

___ _____
___ _____
___ _____

I would feel more important to my dad if I . . .

_____

_____

I would feel more important to my dad if he would . . .

_____

_____

TO MY MOM, I feel more (+), less (-), or equally (=) important than:
___ her work
___ her house
___ her friends
___ her rest/recreation
___ her clothes
___ her relationship with Dad
___ her relationship to God
___ her kitchen
___ her committee work

___ _____
___ _____
___ _____

I would feel more important to my mom if I . . .

_____

_____

I would feel more important to my mom if she would . . .

_____

_____

Some Additional Questions:

I feel really proud of myself when I

_____

_____

_____

I am really good at

_____

I really enjoy

_____

I feel worthless when I

_____

If I could change one thing about myself, it would be

_____

Make It Happen

1. Analyze your daily routine. If there isn't any time for conversation, make some changes. Do you eat meals together? Do you have time right after school? Do you wind down together at bed time? There's opportunity; find the time that's right for you and your children.

2. How do you show your children they are important? If they don't sense your respect and interest, they won't be as free to open up with you.

3. Invite your children's friends over for dinner. Sometimes peer-to-peer conversations can clue you in to things you need to ask your children about later.

4. Read books with your children that address problems they may be facing. If they've had a bad day, read *Alexander & the Terrible, Horrible, No Good, Very Bad Day* by Judith Viorst, and ask your child if he's ever felt like Alexander. If it opens conversational doors, step in. If not, reading the story together at least lets your children know you're sensitive to their feelings.

Chapter 7

HOW CAN I HELP MY CHILD UNDERSTAND COMMITMENTS?
Kathy Peel

Every parent appreciates children who are self-motivated and involved in extracurricular activities. But with some children, there's a fine line between being involved and being over-committed. I learned with my oldest son, John, that you can tell a child is pushing himself too hard when he starts to show physical signs of stress.

During his sophomore year of high school, John got a job cleaning a local real estate office and was making more money than most kids his age. I was really pleased, thinking it would relieve the family budget and look good on his resume. Not only was he trying to hold down his job, he was taking advanced algebra, honors chemistry, advanced American history, and playing tennis.

But I figured he could handle it all. My husband, Bill, and I are high-energy types and John has our genes. But then I noticed he'd come home from work or school and say, "I've got to sleep for a little while. I'm exhausted." He sounded like a forty year old, not a teenager.

Finally John came into our bedroom one day and said, "Mom, I don't think I can take this schedule anymore." I thought, *This kid's under too much stress. He's only sixteen years old—he's got the rest of his life to work.*

By expressing how proud I was of him, I had communicated to him that he should be able to manage all of his activities, when in fact he couldn't. I should have realized he was doing too much before he came right out and told me. Since then I have learned to take the time to analyze my kids' physical well-being, because it serves as a fairly accurate gauge of how well they're coping with their level of involvement.

A Measure of Joy

If you're concerned about your children's level of involvement, watch for their ability to relax and play. Then ask, "When you do all these things that you're into right now, how do you feel at the end of the day?" Their answers will tell you whether they have joy in their lives. Joy is going to leave if a person is involved in too much.

—Gail

If you sense that your child has taken on too many commitments, let him drop some activities, even ones you know he would succeed in. You could also give him the freedom to make a B in a subject instead of an A, even though you're thinking "scholarship, scholarship, scholarship." Allow your children to be who God created them to be, giving them the freedom to choose their activities and set the pace for their level of involvement, rather than imposing your own agenda on them.

Farmers, Not Architects

As parents, we want to see our children do their best and become all that God created them to be, but we've got to realize God created everyone to be unique. What Bill and I try to do is think of ourselves as farmers of our children rather than architects. An architect builds something new. He visualizes something in his mind, and then he designs it, draws it, and builds it. A lot of times we catch ourselves doing that with our children; we try to shape them to fit into our own designs for them.

But a farmer takes a seed and cultivates it. He encourages

what is already inherent in the seed. He doesn't make the squash seed into a cotton plant. But he cultivates a seed with a good environment, the right amount of water, fertilizer, and sunshine.

Maybe we want our child to be a lawyer, but he loves working with his hands. If so, we need to provide him opportunities to work with his hands. Go down to the Goodwill store and buy cheap old appliances and let him take them apart and put them back together. Nurture the talents inherent within him.

Know When to Say No

Although I believe my role as a parent is to help my children reach their full potential, there is, however, a tension between allowing them to cut back busy schedules if they realize they've over-extended themselves and teaching them to stick with their commitments. Somehow we need to communicate two seemingly contradictory truths to our children: one, we live up to our commitments, and two, sometimes it's okay to quit. The deciding factor should be the reasons for wanting to quit.

Inconvenience is not a valid reason. If we aren't willing to work hard to see something through to completion, then it may be time to encourage a child to stick it out. The reward will be a job well done and a new sense of determination. But if a commitment is affecting our child's emotional or physical well-being, it should be looked at in a different light.

> ### Pressure Gauge
> Sometimes the signs of over-commitment or extreme pressure can show up in the parents. If we begin to question whether or not we should be encouraging our child in sports or music, ask, "Is this too important to me? Can I relax?" We need to listen to the child, but it's also necessary to listen to our own motives. Ask, "Why am I doing this? Is it something the child really wants, or is it because of some lack in me that I'm imposing this on my child?"
>
> —Karen

One year, for instance, Joel played in a fall baseball league where they practiced until 9:30 at night. His grades suffered and he was exhausted. We allowed him to quit, and he immediately felt better physically and emotionally, and his grades improved.

By watching our children's physical and emotional health, we should be able to gauge whether they are taking on too many commitments. As we come to know their limitations, we can effectively encourage them to grow in ways that use their talents for God's glory.

Make It Happen

1. Be direct. Ask your children what activities they most enjoy. Ask what they would do if they could do anything in the world. Then ask what they don't like to do. Their answers will help you nurture your children according to their natural bent.

2. Attend as many of your children's activities as possible. Watch for signs of enjoyment or stress. Then if they say they want to quit, you'll be better able to help them come to a decision.

3. Ask why. "What is your reason for wanting to play in the band?" If it's because a best friend is in the band, your children may not stick with the commitment long, especially if the friend leaves for some reason. Check out your children's motivation before they become involved in something and you may be able to avoid conflict down the road.

Section 2

BUILDING
YOUR CHILD'S
FAITH

C hildren are a gift from God; they are his reward," (Psalm 127:3, TLB). When you held your child for the first time, you were probably awed by the wonder of this gift —not to mention a little overwhelmed by the responsibility of parenting. But for Christian parents, these responsibilities go beyond meeting the day-to-day physical needs of our children. Most importantly, they involve nurturing our children's spiritual side.

As we raise our children, often we find our deepest concerns and most essential how-to questions center on the topic of faith. After all, eternity hangs in the balance. We can't casually toss the issue aside—it's much too close to our hearts.

To encourage a budding faith along, we must be intimately involved in the process. But how? The answer lies in creativity, common sense, and patience that God is at work in our children's lives.

Thankfully, Karen and Kathy, with their fresh and clever ideas on passing the faith along, have turned what could be a question mark in your parenting puzzle into a delightful spiritual adventure.

Chapter 8

HOW DO I TURN MY CHILD ON TO GOD?
Karen Mains

T he biggest mistake Christian parents make is to present spiritual life as an obligation rather than a delight. Instead of Christianity being something that's filled with positives, adventure, and excitement, it becomes a dreadful list of "Thou shalt nots." So children view Christianity only from its negative aspects. As parents, we need to show that Christianity is a positive faith—one filled with "can dos."

Those who study human behavior say that 90 percent of everything we learn is caught, not taught. We can't tell our children to pray unless we are doing it. We can't tell our children to give their lives to God unless we are doing it. We can't tell our children to forgive their siblings unless they see us ask for forgiveness. Modeling is as simple as this: we've got to "be" it before we can pass our teaching on.

Moreover, children learn who God is by the way a home is run. If it's a home where there's acceptance, love, and humor, children think that's how God is. But if it's a home where there's rigidity and autocracy, children think God is rigid and unyielding. Approachability, acceptance, justice, fairness, and gentleness—these are characteristics that typify our Father God.

Another way to highlight the positives of our faith is to teach children to delight in God and in his gifts. Take time to notice the world around you, and say to your children, "Isn't this a wonderful world? The fall colors are so beautiful!" Or during a trip to the zoo say, "Look at God's sense of humor. We can see it in the animals—he made some of them so funny!" We don't hear much about God's sense of humor in our theology. But humor is part of the child-likeness we never want to lose and shouldn't rob from our children.

Finishing the Seam

In the book of Exodus, God gave the Levites specific instructions on how to make their robes. For example, the neck was supposed to be finished with seam binding so it wouldn't fray. How wonderful to visualize this great Maker of heaven and earth being concerned about such a small detail.

One day I began to ask, "What are the small details in our lives that might fray if we don't take notice and give thanks for them?" To acknowledge God's actions in not only the large things of life but also the small makes it possible for us to bring closure or "finish the seam," as it were, on that day's experience. If we neglect this, those gifts and incidents fray, and we lose them from conscious thought. And children lose the opportunity to see God's hand in their daily experience.

—Gail

Going on a God Hunt

Christianity becomes a positive experience when we recognize God at work in our lives. My husband, David, and I helped our children by playing a game called "God Hunt." We'd challenge our children to look for God in their everyday lives, using four categories we devised. The first is answered prayer. A child may be concerned about a test or he may have a problem with a teacher. As we prayed with our kids about that situation, and saw God answer, their belief in God was strengthened.

One winter when Randall was in high school, he lost his glasses. He prayed that God would help him find them. Early one spring, there was a sudden thaw. As he was walking home, he found his glasses on the soccer field. As those events happen, you begin to teach a child that God is not only a God of the magnificent, he's a God of the little details of life.

The second category is unexpected evidence of his care. For example, Jeremy took the car one day and the motor died. He couldn't get it started. We live by a major highway, right next to a dangerous curve. If the motor had died there, he could have been in a serious accident. That's God's preservation coming down to a matter of feet. The parent's role is to say, "I see God!"

Those are the spiritual happenings children can see all through life if they're taught to look for them. Even when bad things happen, we can see God's care. The "God Hunt" is a continual search for him in the everyday, and that's one of the ways spirituality comes alive.

The third "God Hunt" category is unusual linkage and timing. Jeremy demonstrated this when it was time to go away for college. He had started a Bible study with kids who were juniors when he was a senior in high school. Even while preparing to go away to college, he felt God was going to do something in the lives of the young people in the Bible study and that he shouldn't leave. So he enrolled at a local junior college instead. It was tempting to say, "We want you in a better school than that," but this was a decision we left up to him.

God verified that choice because we saw some of the kids in the Bible study become Christians, as well as some of their friends and parents. Sometimes it takes a couple of years for linkage and timing to unfold, but when they do, we view God's perfect orchestration at work.

God's help to do his work in the world is the fourth category

Setting the Scene

I want my children to know it's a privilege to talk to God, and so my husband and I strive to show them this by our example. We have had many kinds of quiet times and devotions with the kids. Bill may read a few verses of Scripture or I'll write a special devotional for the kids where I combine Scripture with a quote from a wise person and a little prayer for the family that has something to do with the quote and Bible verse. We also hope the children notice that we get up and write in our prayer journals and have quiet time every morning.

—Kathy

where we recognize his presence among us. We see this all the time with our work in the radio broadcast *Chapel of the Air*. The children have observed it as well. We have to come up with a new idea for every broadcast—six times a week! And there's always provision through a magazine article, a conversation, or an incident that's happened—they are gifts to us to do his work. So the kids have seen that sort of thing happen and have learned to look for it in their own lives.

Instilling children with a desire for spiritual things is similar to Tom Sawyer getting his friends to white wash the fence for him. He made it appear to be so much fun, the other children couldn't resist. If parents communicate by their actions and words that a relationship with Jesus Christ is dynamic and vital, children will want the same for themselves.

Make It Happen

1. Imagine your children having the same kind of relationship with Christ that you have. Is that what you desire for them? If you want more for them, begin seeking more for yourself so your children can follow your example.

2. Encourage your children to go on a "God hunt" and make time to share ways they have seen answered prayer, protection, unusual timing, and enabling to do his work. You could keep a chart with a running tally of "God sightings."

3. Share with your children a special verse from your daily reading. This will illustrate the living quality of God's Word and create in them a hunger to read it for themselves.

4. If your children are young, invest in some Bible story books, cassette tapes, or video tapes that will introduce them to God's Word in a way they can understand. The Read-Aloud Bible Stories series by Kent Puckett, illustrated by Ella K. Lindvall (Moody Press), are excellent for one to four year olds. The *Odyssey* cassettes from Focus on the Family and the *McGee and Me* video series from Focus on the Family and Tyndale House Publishers are worth investing in.

Chapter 9

HOW DO I HELP MY CHILD DEVELOP CHRISTIAN SEXUAL MORALITY?
Karen Mains

I t seems everywhere we turn today, we are bombarded by messages about sexuality—most of which are negative at best. We see it in the women on TV who are portrayed as brash and hateful toward men, and in the men who, in turn, are disrespectful of women and ineffective as fathers. On top of that, we hear daily of sex-related stories—child sexual abuse, teen pregnancies, homosexuality—the list reads like something out of Sodom.

Little wonder our children grow up confused about what it means to be a man or a woman, and what is appropriate sexual behavior. When it comes to shaping our children's sexuality and helping them develop a healthy sexual morality, we need to be more intentional today than ever before. As our children grow they will make their own decisions regarding sex. Yet there are many things we can do to help them make right choices as they grow in their sexual identity.

— ❧ —

Before we begin the work of shaping our children's sexual identities, though, we need to first make sure our own understanding of what it means to be male and female is intact. A healthy sexual attitude means having respect and appreciation for both the sexes. Genesis says God created man and woman in his image, so there are attributes in both genders that reveal God. We become whole, healthy sexual beings when we allow ourselves to display both God-made components.

Contentment Can Speak Volumes

Our culture's lack of distinction in sexual identity can't help but confuse a child. But if I love being a woman and my husband enjoys being a man, won't that speak reams to our children?
—*Gail*

The challenge is defining exactly what "male" and "female" are. For the sake of making distinctions, we can identify certain characteristics, like competitiveness, leadership, and drive as being typical male traits. Female traits usually include nurturing, compassion, and tenderness.

The best way for us to teach our children to recognize and feel comfortable with their sexuality is to model respect and appreciation for all of the traits they possess—both male and female. We can allow boys to show tenderness toward their siblings and girls to be competitive.

Kids pick up on our attitudes about the opposite sex from the way they see us treating our mates. For instance, if the children hear Mom say to Dad, "Honey, I really appreciate it when you take time to listen about my day," you're showing your kids that it's okay for Dad to be tender and thoughtful.

Does the father cherish and support his wife at home, at work, and in her pursuit of goals and dreams? And does she support him? Do they show respect for one another? Do they enjoy one another? Do the kids discover them smooching in the kitchen? That's part of married life, part of family life, and kids need to see appropriate affection between their parents.

Author Charlie Shedd illustrated the importance of displaying affection when he asked children to tell him what their favorite time of day was at home. One eleven-year-old boy wrote that his favorite time was when Dad came home from work and went for the cookie jar. Although cookies were off limits to the children, they weren't off limits to Dad. Then Dad would go over and pat Mom on the bottom, and they would hug. That was the boy's favorite time of the day. A solid, affectionate relationship between parents goes a long way in helping a child develop a healthy sexuality.

The Power of Touch

As parents, we communicate volumes with simple touch. Touch is critical to a child's developing sexuality, too. I'm convinced that one of the reasons the world is rampant with premarital sex and homosexuality is that children grow up starved for appropriate physical touch. If we don't affectionately touch our kids, we deliver them into this overcharged sexual world with a physical hunger.

To make sure my kids got the physical affection they needed, I would give them hugs and back rubs. Or we'd sit on opposite ends of the couch with our feet tucked under each other's bottoms—all natural ways to build touch into the everyday.

Christian counselor and author H. Norman Wright elaborates on the significance of touch between fathers and daughters in his book, *Always Daddy's Girl* (Regal). He says that girls who become promiscuous in adolescence often come from homes where fathers have not been affectionate. Fathers play a critical role in helping their daughters develop their femininity. Whether it's with a smile or a wink, or through loving affection, a father tells his daughter he appreciates the young woman she is becoming through all of these gestures.

Let the Men Be Men

We need to not only affirm our sons' maleness, but we need to celebrate women's femininity. For instance, my husband, Bill, places a lot of importance on treating me like a lady. We taught our sons at an early age that women are uniquely fashioned, they are beautiful, their bodies are special. To encourage my sons' masculinity I'll squeeze their arms and comment on how strong and muscular they are. I thank them when they act like gentleman—whether it's getting my chair at the dinner table or opening a door for me. My femininity helps reinforce their maleness.

—Kathy

No matter how much attention and affection we give our children, we're still fighting an uphill battle against a culture that says sex is everything and approved in any form. Our children are being forced into a world where nearly every type of behavior and lifestyle seems acceptable. Thankfully, we have Scripture to rely on to help us show our children what God intended for relationships in this world.

It's critical that we take the time to read through passages in the Bible that speak to the issues of sexuality, sexual immorality, and its consequences. Although small children are not old enough to comprehend the issue of sex, you can begin shaping their concept of femininity and masculinity by teaching them about the way their bodies are made and how they differ from the opposite sex. Let them know their bodies are temples of God, that they have private parts that are beautiful but are not for anyone else to share. Then as they get older, you can continue this kind of open communication and broaden your discussions to include your children's understanding of sex and morality.

Raising kids in our culture can be a frightening endeavor. Outside influences are powerful, and the consequences of our children's actions with sex can be life-threatening. It takes an extra effort on our part as parents to counter the immoral behavior going on around us and teach our children in no uncertain terms what kind of sexual behavior is God-honoring and what isn't. If we're modeling positive sex roles as man and woman—husband and wife—that will reinforce for our children what Scripture teaches them about relationships.

Although we all want to see our children retain their innocence for as long as possible, ultimately they will make their own choices for their lives. Knowing this, sometimes the best and most significant thing we can do for them is pray—pray that God keeps them in his care and upholds them from the dark influences of this world.

Make It Happen

1. If you and your husband don't show affection in front of the children, talk to your husband about it. Is he uncomfortable with letting other people see him kiss you? There may be some unresolved conflicts you can help him express. Or it may be simply he's never thought about the importance of demonstrating his affection for you in front of the children, but he's more than happy to start doing so.

2. Don't allow your children to grow up starved for physical touch. Shower them with hugs, squeezes, and even a playful punch in the arm. Be careful not to embarrass older children with public affection if they are uncomfortable with it; give them their ration of touch at home.

3. Think through your own "male" traits and thank God for them. Are you a leader in your church? Are you able to be firm with your children when they need it? These qualities bring balance to your life and are part of God's image reflected in you.

4. Make praying for your children a daily priority. Constantly seek God's guidance and wisdom in communicating to them about sex and their developing sexual identities.

Chapter 10

HOW CAN I KEEP MY CHILD INTERESTED IN CHURCH?
Kathy Peel

A s Christian parents we know we have an obligation to nurture our children's faith. One of the
most basic ways we do this is by bringing them to church on a
regular basis. All too often, though, kids fail to see the value of
worship, and Sunday mornings turn into a battle of wills.
Something the founder of Young Life, Jim Raburn, once said
helped me understand the frustration children often feel about
attending church: "It's a sin to bore children with the gospel."

Since hearing this, I have tried to become more sensitive to
my kids' perspective about church. I've determined that parents
basically have three choices regarding their child's church attendance: You can let the child stay home; insist that he or she
attend; or find an alternate church-related activity for their
involvement.

— ❧ —

Early in our parenting, we decided our family's standard
would include church attendance. Not that we're legalistic about
attending every time the doors are open, but "as a rule" we are
there every Sunday we're in town.

I believe when children are very young, up to age twelve, there are some things they don't get to decide. For example, a friend called me once and said, "I'm trying to decide where to put my child in kindergarten. We've visited four schools and now I'm letting him make the choice." I thought, *He isn't responsible to make that kind of choice. You are.* Parents simply have to decide for children that some things, in this case church or Sunday school, are important and your children do them.

Children often ask, "Why do I have to go to church?" You can tell preschoolers, "You will go to church because this is what we do as a family." As they grow you can say, "We go to church because the New Testament tells us we should 'assemble together.' We want to worship God and we want to learn more about him and we can do that at church."

<hr>

If children resist attending church or Sunday school, it's important to find out why. It might be they don't like their Sunday school teacher, and that's a valid argument. I can vividly remember when one of the children was in an early elementary grade, and he disliked his Sunday school teacher. We acknowledged his feelings by saying, "You know there are people in the world that are hard to love. Let's try to stick it out and we'll do some fun things with the class."

You might invite the teacher over for dinner so your child can get to know the teacher on a more personal level. Or, like I once did, you might call the teacher and say, "Our son is having some problems in Sunday school. Is there anything I need to know about?" By offering to help, you come across as willing to be part of the solution.

Then on Sunday morning I'd try to let my son know I understood his feelings. I'd say, "I know this is hard, but it's just for fifty minutes. We'll do something fun this afternoon."

Making Worship Meaningful

Our youngest son, James, still dislikes the idea of having to sit through the adult worship service. The church we attend starts putting children in the adult service at age four, which I felt was a lot to ask of my son when he was four. So every week I packed an activity bag with quiet toys and books. I wanted to make it as pleasant for him as possible, so he didn't build resentment toward church in general.

I believe there is little virtue in making a young child sit through an adult service not geared for preschoolers. That's why children's church services are so important. If there isn't one in your church, maybe you could help start one. Talk to the other parents in your church about rotating the responsibility. If you work together, you can come up with a worship hour that will be meaningful for young children.

These actions might help your children feel better about attending church or Sunday school and, at the very least, show you're sensitive to their problems.

Front and Center

Though a pastor, Gordon made it a point to sit with our children in the front row during worship services, leaving us only to pray and preach. We sat with a child on either side of us, which made is easy for Gordon to touch all of us. He capitalized on the fact that Mark and Kristy loved to have their necks and ears massaged. Gordon's affectionate touches helped our children to connect church with a warm, fuzzy feeling, not a cold, distant experience.

—Gail

A Change of Place

Sometimes we have to take more drastic steps to improve our children's feelings about worship. I can remember once when we were looking for a new church and the boys were unhappy because we couldn't find one everybody liked. We were all feeling a little discouraged, so one Sunday we had our own worship service at a state park. We cooked breakfast, and then we collected stones and built a little altar under a tree and had a family prayer time. We prayed about a lot of things, including our concerns about finding a new church.

I think it's worthwhile to have your own church service on occasion, even when you aren't having problems. Get away to a nice, natural environment so you're not distracted. You can see God in fresh ways through nature. It's also a wonderful time to talk seriously as a family. Be willing, as parents, to hear your children's concerns about life.

As our children entered the teen years, we chose to change churches based on the strength of the youth group. Some people, however, don't have that choice. Small towns often don't have a lot of churches.

That's when parents need to be willing to step in and do what they can to nurture a church youth group. Whether it's opening your home for meetings, providing refreshments, taking the initiative to talk to potential adult sponsors, or sponsoring the group yourself—do whatever you can to strengthen your child's youth group.

Welcome to the Adult World

Sometimes kids are spiritually beyond the classroom level for their age group due to conversations at home about spiritual topics. When the classroom material is below their interest level, kids get bored. When this was the case, we let our kids sit with the adult Sunday school classes when possible. This challenged them spiritually and also showed we respected their insights.

—Karen

A Chance to Serve

Another thing that can change your children's attitude about church is to give them a chance to serve rather than always be served. But, like so many other things, it might take the parent's participation to make it happen.

Our oldest son John didn't enjoy participating in the youth group initially. That was until he was given the responsibility for skits and games for their Wednesday night Bible study. Now every week he comes to me for ideas, but he has to carry them out. In that way I am helping, but not doing the job for him. And he's a lot more interested in attending the group's activities.

Many teenagers and preteens are good at working in the nursery and playing with younger children, and I've never known a church that didn't need people to help in the nursery.

One woman tells the story of a time her child was not

responding to the teaching style of his Sunday school instructor. She and her husband asked him if there was a place he'd like to serve in the church rather than attend Sunday school, and he chose the nursery. So at eleven years old, he went to the nursery to work with the babies and loved it. His parents decided that rather than force their son to do something he hated—and possibly run the risk of turning him off to church all together—they would let him take a break from Sunday school and experience the joy of serving the church. Their solution was a very creative one to a frustrating problem.

Consider the Source

If your children are resisting church attendance, it may be tied to their parents' attitudes. Children can resent church if Mom and Dad are gone too many evenings at church meetings and activities. However, we don't need to go to the extreme of non-involvement either. Find a balance. Everybody has their own capacity for serving and giving and you have to work that out within your own family.

We don't usually go to Sunday evening services. Our attendance depends on the kids' schedules and how much homework they have. Once, Bill and I were asked to speak in an evening service and we didn't make the children attend. Some people might have thought that was strange. Here we were speaking on the family, and our children were not sitting in the audience listening to us. Yet we had been out of town part of the weekend, and they were behind in their homework. We felt it was more important for them to not be stressed out about school than to go hear their mom and dad speak.

— ❦ —

Parents also have to watch their attitude toward problems or personalities at church. If we complain about things at church, our children will more easily develop negative attitudes. Even if they like the church, we might curb their enthusiasm or make them think church isn't going to remain a positive experience as they grow.

Older children will probably pick up on problems within the church. Deal with them honestly, but don't allow yourself to gossip or complain. Encourage them to pray with you that God would bring about resolution to the problems.

— ❧ —

It's inevitable that our children will express some dislike for church or negative attitudes toward Sunday school at some point in their lives. I've found that, rather than overreact to their reluctance to attend worship service, it helps to listen to their complaints so they know we are sensitive to their feelings. Although you may have established rules for church attendance, as we have, you can at least help your children work through their negative feelings and mutually come up with a solution that meets their needs for spiritual development and obedience to God's commands. If you're operating from a true spirit of love, God will help direct your decisions through prayer. And I believe he will give you peace when you've made the right choice.

"Do I Hafta Go?"
Tactics for winning the Sunday morning battle
Naomi DeGroot

The issue of church attendance plagues most families at some time. "It's boring" is the common complaint, but what does boring mean?

For the fourth to sixth grader it may mean, "I'd rather play basketball." For the seventh to twelfth grader, "I don't like Sunday school" often means, "The kids are unfriendly and I don't feel accepted." At any age, "It's boring" can mean what it says: the lessons don't relate to real life, or the teacher is uncommitted and doesn't want to be there either.

At times the problem is minor and requires some good listening on behalf of the parent. Joel is a bright, active fourth grader. Often his request to stay home from church was followed by, "But it's so long."

When his mother began to listen, it didn't take long to discover what was wrong. Joel wasn't rebelling against his parents, church, or God. He just couldn't handle sitting for two-and-a-half hours. Renee found that listening to Joel, praying for wisdom, and letting him run around outside between services took care of a year-long problem.

In the case of older children the problem may be more complex.

"No one spoke to me. It was like I wasn't there," David said.

"If they don't have a friend in the youth group," advises youth pastor Ron Freeborn, "nine times out of ten a child won't attend."

Nurturing friendships is an area where parents can help. If your son doesn't have a buddy at church, invite a family who has a son his age to meet you at the pizza parlor after church. Or, drop your daughter and her church friend off at the mall and arrange for the friend's mom to pick them up.

If helping your teen make friends takes care of Sunday school protests, that's great. But sometimes the problem runs deeper.

Dr. James Dobson reminds parents that children are often cruel to each other. He warns that in a Sunday school classroom where there isn't a strong leader, "students are busily mutilating one another's egos. In fact, it can become the most 'dangerous' place in a child's week."

What can parents do when a child complains about a teacher or the lessons? Allowing them to drop out isn't the only answer. Check out their complaints using biblical guidelines. Are the children of the teacher obedient, and are they believers (1 Timothy 3:4 and Titus 1:6)? Is the teacher a mature Christian with the ability to teach and a person of good reputation (1 Timothy 3:2-7)?

If the teacher checks out okay, what about the lessons? Ask your malcontent what class is like. Or volunteer to help in class and listen with "teen ears." Are teens encouraged? Are they comforted and urged to live lives worthy of God?

Marcia, mother of four teens, is facing these questions. She found that the Sunday school lessons were pure Bible study with no practical applications. Marcia is trying a compromise. On Sunday mornings they go to the family church. On Sunday nights she drives her children fifteen miles to a youth group they enjoy.

There is no one right solution to the issue of church attendance, but there are many options. Finding the best one for your family takes careful listening to your children—and to the Father, who gives wisdom to all who ask.

Whatever approach you choose, your goal is the same. As parents we want to be able to say, "I have no greater joy than to hear that my children are walking in the truth"(3 John 4).

From Today's Christian Woman
(May/June 1989)

Make It Happen

1. Listen to your children's complaints and try to determine the reason for their dissatisfaction. If they complain about Sunday school, sit with them in class for a few Sundays—with the teacher's permission. Then you can intelligently evaluate your children's concerns.

2. Decide what things you're going to insist upon and what things you can be flexible about, like what your children can wear.

3. Attend a church that's good for your children. Do what you can to make church a positive.

4. Make sure your own attitude about church is positive. Guard your tongue. Don't spend the ride home from church bad-mouthing the minister, the sermon, or the people sitting in front of you in church. Children will pick up on your negativism.

5. Evaluate your level of involvement. Are you spending too much time in church-related activities, tempting your children to resent church? Are you only a pew-warmer, communicating to your children that church has little to offer? Find a level of involvement that will properly communicate to your children the place church should have in their lives.

Chapter 11

HOW DO I SHOW MY CHILD GOD IS AN ANSWER TO OVERCOMING HIS FEARS?
Kathy Peel

When my son John was five, he was petrified to go down a high slide at the park. He was my first child and I wanted him to be proficient in everything. But his fear of the slide soon had me thinking, *Something is wrong with my child. He's probably the only five year old in the world that won't go down the slide.* I made special trips to the park just to help him work through his fear. I told him, "You're going to learn how to go down the slide. Every five-year-old should be able to do this." Finally, after numerous frustrating attempts, I left him alone. Eventually he went down the slide by himself.

This was one of my first lessons in understanding what a child needs most in overcoming fears—time and compassion. The longer I'm a mother, the more patient I try to be with my children's fears. I try to acknowledge their fears and say, "Yes, I understand." I try to help them talk about their feelings, not suppress them.

I remember when John was sixteen and I applied the "let him work it out" approach to his fears as a new driver. The very day he got his driver's license he drove to the pizza parlor. The parking lot was a tight squeeze and he backed into another car.

Needless to say, he became fearful of parking lots.

After that experience his criteria for deciding whether or not to go someplace was determined by the size of the parking lot. And he especially avoided that fateful pizza parlor. For a month or two he'd say, "Well, I want to go there, but I don't know where I'd park." Then I noticed about four months later he went back to the same pizza parlor and he parked without a problem. His desire to be independent was stronger than his fear of parking. With time, he overcame his fear on his own. I didn't have to force the issue.

Getting to the Source

One way to counteract a child's fear is to find out the basis for it. Often it stems from something they've seen on television. I firmly believe that the media instills unnecessary fears into our children. I am adamant about not allowing my kids, especially when they were younger, to watch scary television shows or movies. Television programs we, as adults, consider harmless can upset a child. One woman told me how a medical rescue show upset her daughter. The program depicted paramedics rescuing people from hazardous situations. After her daughter watched one episode, she was unable to sleep until the family discussed what to do in case of a house fire. After that her daughter wasn't permitted to watch the program because she was personalizing what she saw on the screen. By controlling those things that create or feed fear—like the media—we can counteract some of our children's fears.

Scripture tells us to think about things that are lovely, pure, noble, and right (Philippians 4:8). You can give your child a mental advantage over fear by helping fill her mind with wholesome,

Power of Prayer

Each morning, I made a point to ask my kids, "How can I support you today?" It was a way for me to share their stress and offer them comfort and courage during weak moments. For instance, my son Mark dreaded taking tests. I understood his fear because I used to panic before an exam, too. One night before a big test, we talked about how vulnerable he felt. By letting him know I used to fear the same thing, and telling him I would be praying for him, he felt less afraid of failing because he knew he wasn't alone.

—Gail

encouraging thoughts. One mother puts this principle into action by encouraging her ten-year-old daughter to think of her mind as a TV set when she is overcome with a certain fear. She can dwell on what's frightening her, or she can "change the channel." After they have had a chance to discuss the girl's fear, the mother encourages the girl to think about positive, happy things, like a favorite vacation or a book she enjoyed.

Spiders in the Bananas

A lot of childhood fears surface because children are misinformed and easily believe what older friends or siblings tell them. When I was in kindergarten, a girl in our neighborhood told me the black lines in the middle of a banana were crushed-up spider legs. I was in high school before I ate a banana!

Taking time to educate our children can alleviate many fears. For instance, we live in tornado country. A tornado passed near us once, and it was frightening. Afterward, one of the boys kept asking, "Does that cloud look like it's a tornado cloud?" We told him what a "tornado cloud" looks like. And we talked to him about what to do when a tornado comes. We couldn't promise a tornado wouldn't strike, but we could take some of the fear out of the event by preparing him for it.

> ### Invitation to Angels
> At bedtime each night I would deliberately try to insert prayers of well-being into my children's consciousness. We would thank God for what is beautiful and holy, and we would invoke the angels to come and fill their dreams with their presence and fill the room with their protection. That set the stage for peaceful dreams rather than nightmares.
>
> —Karen

In time we went on to discuss other situations: What would you do if a stranger came to the door, if the house caught fire, or if someone choked? By reviewing what should be done in a crisis, we help eliminate some of the fear associated with it.

A God Who Protects

I have also learned that Scripture and prayer can have a powerful influence over a child's ability to overcome fear. A friend of mine remembered her sister using a Bible verse to calm her child-hood fears. She would say Hebrews 13:5 while tapping on her knuckles: "I will never leave you nor forsake you." And it helped.

Old Testament Bible stories may offer the most potent reminder to our children that our God is a sovereign God. Author Jay Kesler says that when a child reads about God parting the Red Sea, making the sun stand still, and closing the mouths of lions, a child can figure, *If God did that, then surely he can take care of me.*

Our children need to know that "God did not give us a spirit of timidity, but a spirit of power . . ."(2 Timothy 1:7). The more we can teach them to rely on Scripture and prayer in con-fronting their fears, the more likely they are to successfully over-come them on their own—and in their own time.

Battling the Boogeyman
Judith Monroe

Many children use security devices to escape their fears. But many also entertain fear as a friend because it gains them extra attention or saves them from disagreeable tasks. Have you ever placed unpleasant phone calls for your children, or interfered in conflicts they could have solved? We tend to over-protect our children. But our loving overprotection may eventually produce emotional cripples who refuse to confront their fears. A wise mother gradually moves out of the role of "fear facer."

James Dobson, in *Preparing for Adolescence*, suggests that fear can limit our behavior to those acts that are completely safe and totally beyond ridicule. We need to encourage our children to be risk takers.

But risk-taking, like fear-facing, develops gradually. In the long run the fear of doing something we're afraid of is not as painful as avoiding it. A fear faced becomes less threatening. We need to encourage our children to talk about their fears. Children who are unable to verbalize their fears can draw pictures or act them out.

If your children are young, consider singing to them as you tuck them in at night. The joy of singing, especially when you're sad or afraid, is a priceless gift to give to your children.

Encourage your children to keep a record of fears they have overcome. "Remember when? . . ." will help to provide strength against new foes.

Your children's minds are sponges. Help them soak up messages of love and faith to draw upon in times of stress. Memorized Bible passages from a translation they can understand wield great power over a mind paralyzed with fear. Instead of defeatist phrases like, "I'm afraid of storms," your children can focus on comforting words like these:

"Do not be afraid—I am with you! I am your God—let nothing terrify you! I will make you strong and help you; I will protect you and save you" (Isaiah 41:10, Good News).

Children who are led into friendship with God live with a quiet assurance of his protection. They learn to leave their fears in God's hands. As one person put it, "My fear is gone in the great quiet of God."

Adapted from Today's Christian Woman
(September/October 1988)

Make It Happen

1. Try to remember what frightened you as a child. When your children relate their fears, tell them what you used to be afraid of. That will help them realize that fears are a normal part of growing up and they will eventually get over them.

2. Show compassion for your children's fear. If they are afraid of the dark, don't plunge them into a dark room to force them to get over their fear. Instead, try putting a night light in the room, or lay down with them for a few nights until they go to sleep. This validates that emotions like fear are okay.

3. Help give your young children a language for the emotion they feel. Ask, "What are you feeling?" and then say, "That is called anger," or "That is fear."

4. Do you owe one of your children an apology? If you didn't take them seriously when they told you about a fear, they could be hurt and unable to talk to you about it. Take the initiative and clear the air so you can help them face their fears.

Chapter 12

WHAT IF MY CHILD REJECTS THE FAITH?
Karen Mains

One of the greatest concerns for Christian parents is that our children turn their backs on the faith. And when something like this does happen, it's easy to overreact and further exacerbate the situation. While I have not experienced the heartache of a child rejecting Christianity, there was a time when our teenage daughter didn't want to attend extended family functions with us. This was distressing to me, and it helped me understand the pain a parent—and especially God—feels when a child leaves the fold.

In our case our daughter, Melissa, would become extremely tense before family gatherings. I consulted a trusted friend who is also trained as a counselor, and she said, "Something is obviously wrong, and you need to give Melissa permission to say no. If you give her permission to say no, eventually, she will give herself permission to say yes."

"But how do we explain to the family that Melissa's not coming?" I asked. My friend's advice was simple yet wise. "If they ask you, tell them to ask Melissa," she said.

Eventually, Melissa resolved her inner struggles and resumed her involvement with the extended family. By allowing her to stay home during holiday parties and other family functions, we affirmed Melissa's ability to make her own choices and we showed her we respected her distress. If we had continued to deny her pain, she might have continued saying no. As it was, she was able to work her way through her struggle because there was no pressure from us.

Similarly, parents need to tell their doubting child it's okay to struggle spiritually, to question their faith. They need to say, "Many people go through this. This is part of being human. Of course, we want for you to know the Lord, but we will all learn many things from your doubting."

Rather than spending energy in arguments or putting the child down, affirm everything you can. Agree that it is hard to coordinate the resurrection accounts. Acknowledge that Christians are often hypocritical. You can even affirm the child's right to question and the desire to turn away.

That's essentially the story of the prodigal son. The father gave the son his inheritance, let him choose his own way, waited for him to return home, and welcomed him back.

Wooed Back Home

The best thing I can do for children who wander from the faith is what God does for me: he gives me the ability to choose. But if I choose to leave him, he woos me back. He woos me through prayer. Jesus is at the right hand of God praying for us (Romans 8:34).

—Karen

The beauty of the way the father of the prodigal son responded is that, while he released his son to the consequences of choices made, his heart and arms were eagerly open, not closed by self-righteousness or anger. This made it possible for the son to come to the place of "homesickness" for the presence of his father.

If this is not true, and love is conditional, and the door to our home and heart is tightly shut, homesickness probably won't occur. Who is drawn to a home like that? There has to be something redemptive and more loving about home and our Father than what the world offers.

Did I Do Something Wrong?

Most parents of prodigal children go through a terrible phase of asking, "What have we done wrong?" It's possible you didn't do anything to cause your child to leave the faith. Every person has a will of his own and despite our best efforts, our children sometimes make wrong choices.

But very often there is something in the way we operate as a family or something in the church that is not healthy and has contributed to our children's choices. For instance, if children do not feel free to ask questions about the family's or church's beliefs, they eventually may be driven to break free from that environment. If negative consequences are the result of asking honest questions about one's faith, children very likely may come to hold a negative view of that faith.

Additionally, parents sometimes come to love their children for their performance rather than for who they are. Often this is subtle, but it shows when we withhold affection from them when they disappoint us, or increase our affection when their behavior pleases us. Love should be given regardless of action, good or bad. Children reared in a home where love is conditional may decide to test God's love for themselves.

> ### Eating with the Pigs
> Even though we gladly welcome our children home when they stray from the faith, that's not to say we make the life of rebellion easy by eliminating the consequences of their choices. As a friend of mine pointed out, the father of the prodigal son didn't go after his boy with McDonald's hamburgers; so, too, we need to let our children "eat with the pigs" to bring them to their senses. By releasing them without rancor and allowing them to feel the full weight of their choices, we will be far more likely to woo them home to us and the Lord we represent.
> —Gail

When to Get Help

If a child rejects both the faith and his parents, I would suggest the parents get professional help. It's like dealing with a problem marriage. Even if only one partner will get help, the marriage can improve. In this case, you can find out what *you* can change about yourself so you're not contributing to the problem. You can't change your child or "bring him back" by your own effort. That is your child's choice. But you can learn new ways to cope with the loss and disappointment you may feel.

Just as I learned from the experience with our daughter Melissa, sometimes the best thing you can do for wandering children is let go of them. Let them go their own way without trying to hold them back. That seems like a cruel thing to do, but in fact, it's loving. If I had tried to force Melissa to be an active member of the family during a time when she was feeling unable to participate, I would have run the risk of creating deep resentment in her toward us and the rest of the family. And, like my counselor/friend told me, don't attempt to explain your child's behavior to other people. Instead say, "I'd rather not try to speak for John. Maybe you'll have the opportunity to talk to him about it sometime."

— ❦ —

Sometimes letting children wander on their own is necessary to bring them to the end of themselves and back to God. And ultimately, our children's decision to follow the faith or leave it is one they will have to answer to God for on their own. If we have done all we can to nurture our children's faith, then, as parents, we need to trust they will make the right choice and come home when the time is right.

Are You Raising a Spiritual Drop-Out?
Holly Green

My husband and I are proud of our children and want them to succeed because we love them. But we also have selfish motives. Our own feelings of accomplishment are enhanced by the achievements of our offspring. Among Christians, this drive often carries over into the spiritual realm. We are eager to see our children blossom spiritually. But in our zeal we sometimes assume we have more control over this than we actually do. We try to manipulate our children into the Kingdom and place pressures on them they cannot handle. To turn down the heat and not push too hard there are several things we can do:

Allow your children to be different from you. Teens especially need to establish a faith of their own. Don't expect to produce spiritual clones. Instead of trying to teach our kids all the 'right' Christian words, we spent many evenings and mealtimes discussing spiritual matters and asking for their opinion and expecting their perspective to be different. We often disagreed but we never belittled.

Allow your children to be different from each other. A retired pastor, father of five children, three of whom are not close to the Lord, confesses, "The biggest mistake I made was treating all my children the same. I assumed what worked well for the oldest, who was very compliant, would be equally effective for the other four. I was wrong." The key to stimulating spiritual growth is knowing what captivates the heart and mind of each child.

Give reasons for your rules. One couple has two sets of

household rules. "We wanted to make sure our two daughters understood that some requirements were ours, not necessarily God's," explains the mother. "So we had Family Rules and God's Laws. Lying was against God's Laws. Wearing a bikini was against Family Rules. Rules were devised by humans and therefore open to discussion and revision. God's Laws were not."

Be flexible in the ways you introduce your children to God. Family spiritual routines need to change as your children age. Watch for signs of dissatisfaction and be ready to make adjustments as required. When our boys began to "hate" church, we found in talking to them they were starved for Christian friends. In our small church there was only one other girl in their Sunday school class.

From Today's Christian Woman
(May/June 1990)

Make It Happen

1. Allow your children to discuss their spiritual questions and doubts. You might want to initiate discussions, ask what your children believe about God, and invite their questions.

2. Examine your own walk with God. If your beliefs contradict your behavior, your children will have reason to doubt the validity of what you teach.

3. Sometimes it's difficult to express our concerns to our children when all their responses are hostile. Consider writing a letter to your children, telling them what's on your mind. Avoid preaching—just tell your children what you're feeling and what you wish for your relationship. Reaffirm your love.

Section 3

BUILDING YOUR PARENTING SKILLS

Parenting is tough enough. But our multiple expectations make it even tougher. After all, we know the potential God has in store for parenting our children and so we set our sights high.

But what is realistic when it comes to plotting our hopes and dreams for parenting? How can we "do it all" if we have a husband who chooses not be an active participant in parenting, or we are a single parent? How can we promote an atmosphere of brotherly love if the kids argue endlessly? And how can we do anything if we're caught in the tug-of-war between balancing marriage, parenting, and work?

In the following chapters Gail, Karen, and Kathy offer wise, compassionate—and practical—advice on how to keep the day-to-day realities of life from robbing you of your dreams.

Chapter 13

HOW CAN I BALANCE THE DEMANDS OF PARENTING, MARRIAGE, AND WORK?
Gail MacDonald

There is probably no greater stress on a mother than feeling torn between husband and children. Add a job to the mix, and your stress level may go off the charts. The first step toward reducing the pressure that comes from trying to fill several roles is to assess your expectations. Ask yourself: What is my definition of a good wife and mother? And, given the busy circumstances of my life, is it possible for me to meet these expectations?

When you are working—even part-time, or from your home—you and your husband need to face facts and adjust your expectations. It just is not realistic to expect to do everything, everyday that perhaps a stay-at-home mom might be able to do. Does your husband expect a home-cooked, three-course dinner each evening? If you have preschoolers, do you expect to have a spotlessly clean house? Expectations such as these may have to be scaled back or even abandoned for a time.

Identifying expectations and weighing them against the realities of the daily schedule is a task you and your husband should take up together. You need to set aside time to ask, "How many blocks of time do we have to be together each week?

97

When are we all together as a family? What can we put into those times, and what do we expect to get out of them?"

Doing this won't eliminate that overwhelmed feeling, but it may bring a measure of calm and control to your life. It's also helpful to remember that the demands on you as a mother will change over time. During the first months of a baby's life, the family usually helps out a great deal with the many demands of a newborn. Over time, though, as your baby moves through infancy and toddlerhood and then becomes involved in school-age activities, his demands on your time and energy will not be as great. You and your husband need to keep this in mind during the more hectic days.

Putting the Marriage First

While we sometimes have to scale back our expectations in certain areas of our lives, one expectation worth holding on to is that of developing a strong marriage. It's important for each of us as wives and mothers to remember that children are a gift and a blessing to marriage, but they are not essential to a marriage. Their arrival does not supersede or replace the relationship between husband and wife. Love for our children comes from the overflow of love between husband and wife.

Getting together as a couple in the midst of all the chaos can become a habit that enhances the health of the marriage. And it's a good reminder to everyone in the family, parents as well as children, that the marriage is the key relationship.

When our children were still at home, Gordon and I would schedule a daily debriefing—just the two of us. Without saying a word, we made a statement to our children that the primary relationship in this home is not child to parent, it's husband to wife. If Gordon and I didn't work on what was going on between us, then the children wouldn't have experienced any overflow. They learned to accept those private debriefings, and they found great security in them. Furthermore, that made mealtime a place where the children's interests were the topic of conversation, not adult issues.

At the same time, kids need to know that we value time with them as well. It was always comforting for our children to look in their dad's weekly planner and see Family Day scheduled for weeks, even months, ahead. In black and white, they saw they were an important priority in their dad's life.

Praying on the Go

Maybe you are still clinging to the expectation that you need extended prayer time or Bible study time every day, just as you did before life got so busy. Realistically, though, this is another expectation that may have to be scaled down for a time. When you have small children at home and a job, you need to recognize that during this period in your life you might only be able to grab quick snatches from the Bible and pray on the go. There's nothing wrong with this. The important thing is to remain centered in Christ.

> ## Spinning Wheels
> *With limited time and energy, we need to study and learn what attitudes and actions really communicate to our spouses that we care. If we don't take the time to do this, chances are we'll be spending our efforts on the wrong things.*
>
> *—Kathy*

To me, the Christ-centered person is one who always asks the question, *How would Jesus react to this situation? How would Jesus handle this person? What would his attitude be?* The more we ask for his presence in our lives, the more like him we become.

Being Christ-centered does not require long hours of intensive Bible study. Instead, you could find a way to take just ten minutes out of your morning schedule to get one nugget from the Word or from a devotional book, and then chew on it the rest of the day. You don't even have to set aside the time—just read while you eat your breakfast, or even during your commute to work.

Don't Let Guilt Be Your Guide

When we come into God's presence, even if it's only for ten minutes, we need to come with a sense of desire, not guilt. If we want to spend time with the Lord and we can't, then our longing turns to homesickness. But what often happens to the hassled mom is that she begins to operate from a point of guilt. This is truly counterproductive in our walk with Christ. No one should come to Christ cringing like a child who feels he's failed.

Delight in the Moment

When my husband, David, and I were in the inner-city pastorate, I felt pulled in a million directions. Finally, I reached my breaking point, and I learned then I had limits. And I learned a spiritual principle as well: the more I prayed about the confusing elements in my life, the more God would bring order to my days. Some describe this as the sacrament of the present moment—living fully in the moment you are in and cherishing it. It's a terrible thing to be at work and worrying about your children, and in a sense it's a spiritual sin. When we begin to wear with joy the hat we have on at a particular moment, we experience God's peace and a wonderful sense of freedom in our lives.

—Karen

Just minutes in God's presence allows us to center our day and ourselves in him. We can tell him what's on our minds: "What does Christ have to say to me this morning? Why am I feeling so hassled?" By offering him our hassles and our frustrations, we put God back in charge of our lives. It only takes a moment to open our hearts and say, "Lord, give me heaven's perspective on what's happening right now."

When I had young children and felt pulled in a million directions, I often used a phrase from Charles Wesley. He would say, "May I do nothing today without calmness of soul." Repeating that phrase reminded me of God's presence and had an immediate calming effect on me.

───※───

It's easy to believe that we're the first generation to live at such a breakneck pace, yet Francois Fenlon, a seventeenth-century French writer, addressed this issue in a letter to a woman who felt extremely harried. He wrote, "If you are unable to secure much time to yourself, be all the more careful about stray moments. Even a few minutes gleaned faithfully amid engagements will be more profitable in God's sight than whole hours given up to him at freer seasons. Moreover, many brief spaces of time through the day will amount to something considerable at last."

We, too, need to call upon God and practice his presence in our busiest moments. Only then can we sort out the demands that tug at us and gain a clear picture of what is most important.

I love a statement a mother of seven once said to me. "It takes maturity to deal with the obscurity of motherhood," she said. When you feel so overwhelmed by endless demands, and when you feel as if you're not getting enough attention from anyone, you need to step back and recollect what a wonderful responsibility God has given you. Yes, it means a lot of obscurity. No one may seem to appreciate the five lunches you packed last week, or the kitchen floor you scrubbed twice. But ultimately, the maturity we gain in coping with all the challenges of being a mom is what allows us to find our self-worth in Christ, not in how much we get done each day. It means finding a way to order our days and preserve our emotional health. That is how we learn to find the freedom and the wisdom to weigh our competing demands and respond to them appropriately—like a good mom and a good wife.

Make It Happen

1. Define a "good wife" and "good mother" based on your circumstances. Decide what your priorities should be and adjust your schedule to make time for the most important things. Eliminate the less important things from your life.

2. Don't go it alone. Seek out friends or relatives who might be able to help you when you're especially overburdened. Someone to watch the children for a couple of hours, someone who could make a double-sized meal and let you freeze half for your family.

3. Pray every day. Just before you get out of bed, acknowledge the God who gives you breath, who enables you to face every day, who gives your life purpose. This will help keep your perspective on track.

4. Write a one sentence prayer, or adopt one, such as Charles Wesley's: "May I do nothing today without calmness of soul."

5. Discuss the demands you feel as a wife and mother with your husband. Together you can try to come up with ways to ease the tension. Try to find out where your time is best spent in meeting your husband's needs.

Chapter 14

HOW DO I HANDLE CONFLICT WITH MY HUSBAND OVER OUR DIFFERING DISCIPLINING STRATEGIES?
Gail MacDonald

The time to deal with our dissimilarities in child rearing is long before we find ourselves in the heat of conflict. Early discussions regarding our varying backgrounds as well as studying how each child responds to differing kinds of discipline is key. For instance, some personalities learn best from spanking, others do not. Knowing what will bring the desired response without damaging the relationship is imperative.

Gordon was a necessary balance to me in disciplining our children because he is a "big picture" person. I would tend to isolate the situation, seeing it as an end in itself, while he would see it in the context of the past, present, and future. Once I saw the great genius of this, I worked hard to see the "forest" and not just the "trees."

As parents you may have different ways of viewing an incident that requires discipline, but you can still agree on an overall strategy for parenting. It might be helpful to take some time together to discuss what your long-range goals are for your children. Stated very simply, your goal as Christian parents might be to see your children fulfill all of their God-given potential. Once you've agreed as a couple what your ultimate hope is for your

103

children, then you can begin to map out how you will go about attaining the goal. When parents consider these broader issues of parenting and then strategize together, it helps them put the minor conflicts they have with their children in perspective. With long-range goals in mind, you can recognize that each situation is not an end in itself; it's one part of directing your children toward becoming all that God calls them to be.

Conviction Over Personal Preference

Even so, your parenting skills and those of your husband are influenced to a large extent by how you were raised, as well as by the differences in your personalities. So agreeing on long-range goals gives you a foundation to build on, but it does not guarantee 100 percent agreement on every issue of discipline.

One way to sort out disagreements is to determine which of you holds stronger views on a particular issue. When I was in college, a psychology professor said something I have remembered all these years: "Personal preference should yield to conviction."

For example, I firmly believed that our children should discipline themselves to do their shopping during the weekdays and keep Sunday free of spending. It seemed to me that Scripture was quite clear on the fact that we need a break from spending to consider the value of money and our ability to control ourselves. While Gordon was not as strongly convinced about this in our earlier years, he went along with it, saying, "Let's do our shopping on other days, unless it's an emergency. Mom and I would like us to try hard to make Sunday unique and not like any other day."

In this case, everybody won. Our children learned to ask hard questions about self-discipline and what their future convictions should be, and Gordon and I were able to be united in our response.

— ❧ —

When parents lock horns over disciplining issues, often it's because they aren't in agreement over how strict to be with the children. One parent might say children shouldn't date until they're sixteen, while the other believes it's okay to permit dating as young as thirteen. One way to get around these types of disagreements is to agree to start out with somewhat stricter rules, but then agree to relax the rules to fit the child. Common sense says it is easier to enforce rules in the beginning than it is to get tough later on when certain freedoms have come to be expected.

When issues come up that have you and your husband pointing fingers and calling each other names like "softy," you need to talk it over as soon as possible—and in private. It's okay—even desirable—to let children see you and your spouse disagree and deal with conflict constructively. But they should not see you arguing over what to do about *them*.

The Trouble with Taking Sides

Even more devastating is the situation where one parent sides with the children against the other parent. The wife might go to the children and say, "I disagree with your dad, but let's face it, we're just not going to get him to change." That sort of put-down plants seeds of insecurity in children. If your children see agreement and unity, they feel their parents' marriage is solid and their relationship is healthy. If a wife puts down her husband, the children begin to question the stability of the marriage.

When you do come up against conflict over specific issues

A Good Difference

In Delores Curran's book, Traits of a Healthy Family *(Harper & Row), she agrees that parents need to be consistent. Yet, she says, children are very smart. If Mom and Dad have very different ways of disciplining, children are able to recognize that and live with it. As long as the parents accept one another's different approaches and are not living in tension, it will not damage the children. In fact, it may be good for the family. It illustrates the fact that different people have different ways of solving the same problem.*

In our family, our children have seen my husband, David, and I disagree over how to handle disciplining. We've allowed them to see that we have some areas of disagreement to work through. But with that, they also know that in the end we mutually agree on how to handle the problem and back each other up on the decision.

—Karen

of discipline, first, make a commitment to reach agreement. Reading books or listening to tapes about parenting will give you suggestions for handling specific disciplining problems. The two of you can identify together which methods or suggestions you will use and then implement whichever plan you've chosen. Otherwise, children will quickly detect uncertainty, and they'll play one parent against the other.

Second, take time to really understand your spouse. In order to get along with your husband, who has different ideas about discipline, you need to get to the root of your disagreements. And often the way to do this is to understand how your husband's personality differs from yours.

For example, some people make quick decisions, others are slower and more deliberate. In my marriage, I'm more likely to say, "I want this changed or decided on now. I can't stand this decision being left up in the air." Gordon, on the other hand, tends to make decisions more slowly. Neither style is better. In fact, both have worked in our favor.

Body Language

Bill and I have worked out a little signal to let each of us know when we disagree with the discipline the other is using. If he feels like I'm overreacting or being too harsh, he'll come up to me and put his arm around me. That's his way of letting me know he thinks I need to settle down. And I'll do the same for him. That touch from the other partner tells us we need to discuss the situation in private and work out a mutual solution.

—Kathy

For instance, when Kristy was in sixth grade, I went on a field trip with her class as room mother. I came home highly agitated about some of the friends she seemed to be close to. I knew that if I confronted her about it, I would come down too hard, making rules that would serve only to make me feel better. So I called my husband, who was not emotionally involved, and he was able to handle the situation by drawing out Kristy's attitude toward these friends. Gordon got her to discuss her fears that these friends were not good for her and he found out that she didn't know how to change things on her own. He showed her that we could be her excuse if she wanted one. She could simply tell her friends that her mom and dad said she couldn't play anymore.

She felt such relief! Kristy felt heard and understood. My way would have alienated her because I would have forced her into a defensive posture to prove herself rather than help her identify how she really was feeling.

For Gordon, disciplining is a process. He gathers as much information as he can before he makes a decision about how to handle a situation. Although there have been times when we needed to make a quick decision and Gordon would defer to me, more often than not, his style elicited the best results.

To place value judgments on our different disciplining styles—saying one is good or bad—is unwise. Our differences complement our relationships if we see them as assets. The key to deciding whose style works better is to consider the child and the circumstances that warrant discipline. Sometimes this means Mom's way of handling the situation would be more effective. Other times the husband's perspective may work better in disciplining a child.

Always Growing, Always Changing

Early in our marriage, it was very hard for me to admit that I was wrong when Gordon and I had a conflict. I could get on my knees and ask our young son Mark to forgive me whenever "Momma made a mistake." But with Gordon it was another story. A lot of it had to do with my own insecurity. It sounds almost ridiculous now, but I couldn't help but wonder: If Gordon knew I was so fallible and made mistakes, would he dump me? Fortunately for me, Gordon showed me how to admit wrong by modeling repentance himself. But it took me years to overcome this weakness.

When it comes to working out a strategy for parenting, all too often husbands and wives find themselves reviewing past behaviors. That's fine, as long as we're not using these occasions to blame one another or point out each other's mistakes. Instead, if each of us recognizes and respects the other's areas of vulnerability, we can grow together as parents.

Graciously, Christ never took a snapshot of us in life and said, "There, that's the way you'll always be." But rather, he sees us in video, ever growing and becoming. And that's the way we need to see ourselves, our husbands, and our children, too. When different parenting styles threaten to divide you, it helps to remember that our spouse is approaching the task of disciplining from his unique point of view. Just as you are growing in your role as a mother, so, too, is he developing his skills as a father. Learning to appreciate the special traits he brings to the family will help you better understand how you can work as a team in raising your children. In the long run, your different parenting styles will no doubt complement each other, and offer your children flexible disciplining that is most effective for each of their unique temperaments.

Make It Happen

1. Map out a parenting strategy by mutually establishing your long-range goals for your children and how you are going to help them reach those goals. Describe the character qualities you would like your children to possess and how you can pass those on to them.

2. Consider taking an evening where you and your husband describe the discipline methods your parents used. What did they do that you would like to emulate? What would you like to do differently? This will help you understand each other's point of view and then come up with guidelines that are your own.

3. Work at becoming a consistent "repenter." Learn to say, "I'm sorry" to your husband and your children. Likewise, when conflict over disciplining differences threatens to pull you apart as a parenting team, remember that each of you is in process as a parent. Offer forgiveness to your spouse when you feel hurt by disagreements you may have over disciplining. Try to see your spouse through the eyes of Christ—as a unique, growing person who is doing his best to honor the Father in his role as a parent.

4. Consider coming up with a sign that tells you or your partner you disagree with the method of disciplining the other is using. That way, if you are too emotionally involved in the situation, your husband can hold you accountable and offer a more objective perspective on the situation.

Chapter 15

HOW CAN I GET MY HUSBAND MORE INVOLVED IN PARENTING?
Kathy Peel

Even though fathers today generally are more involved in family life than ever before, many dads still need direction in how to be a team player in the parenting process. If you feel frustrated or disappointed over your husband's lack of involvement at home, it may help to look at some of the reasons why he isn't meeting your expectations.

Many times men don't participate in child rearing because they don't know what to do. It's not that they don't love their children or care about their wives. They're just clueless as to what needs to be done. Often husbands don't get more involved in parenting because they don't realize the impact their fathering has on the children.

One of the challenges we face in getting our husbands to respond to our requests for help is to give him compelling reasons for him to be involved. There are a number of critical reasons why our husbands should be involved in the parenting of our children, such as a father's affirmation or the male viewpoint on certain situations. But if they don't sense the significance of those reasons, then it will be difficult to get them to respond favorably to our requests for help.

Before you embark on a full-scale mission to get your husband more involved with the kids, first take some time to show you respect and understand his situation. A lot of times men come home with work still on their minds. They need time to make the adjustment to being a family man. If he's a talker, give him time to unload. Listen and ask questions to help him think through the events of his day. If he's quiet, give him uninterrupted time to unwind before being bombarded with kids and home.

Of course, the tension nowadays, especially with 65 percent of mothers working outside the home, is that both Mom and Dad face the same dilemma. Both need time to shift gears from being at work to coming home. If this is true for you, your situation can actually serve as a way to get your husband involved with the family because you'll need to develop a system that gives you both time to make the switch from work to home. Just as you try to accommodate his needs at the end of the work day, so, too, he can take responsibility for helping you cope with your competing time demands.

Turning Duty into Delight

A critical factor in approaching our husbands about helping out more with the kids is to be positive. If he feels nagged into doing something, it's going to be a chore—a duty rather than a delight. Granted, he does have responsibility, but using encouragement and praise will serve as far better motivators.

Rather than nagging ("Why don't you ever do that?"), or using the martyr's approach ("I have to do everything. I wish you'd help every once in a while!"), try to let him know how much you value his help so he feels appreciated. Tell him, "You have so much to offer the children." Name some of the positive qualities the kids could pick up from him just by hanging around their dad.

For instance, Bill is good at improving things and finding practical ways of getting things done. He's the kind who would say, "Let me help you figure out how to get into this computer program," or "We really can't afford to buy a new bike, so let me help you refurbish this old one." I try to make it a point to let him know how much I admire his resourcefulness and how happy I would be to see our kids learn some of what he knows. This way he's more likely to see the value in spending time with the children.

Mind Games

One trap that's easy to fall into is expecting our husbands to be mind readers. Let's face it, if we want them to do something, we need to let them know what it is we need their help with. Be specific. Ask, "Honey, could you call out spelling words for Junior at 7:30?" or "After the rest of the kids go to bed, could you talk to Julie about the struggle she's having with her history teacher?" Asking for his help with specific tasks may get a better response than just asking for "a little help around here."

Going Solo

Sometimes we have to create circumstances where Dad takes care of the kids on his own. For instance, one time I had to travel for several weeks. I would call home every night to find out how things were going. Of course, I assumed everything would fall apart without me. But David would say, "We're having the most wonderful time."

I realized then that even though he didn't handle every situation as I would have wanted him to, he was still doing a capable job. I think sometimes the reason husbands aren't more involved at home is because we ask them to do something and then we get upset when they don't do it our way. And when we interfere, we undermine the very thing we've asked them to do and be.

—Karen

Know Your Strengths and Weaknesses

If your husband has been pretty much uninvolved up to this point, it's probably unrealistic to expect him to take over all responsibility for the children when he gets home, even though you've had the kids all day, or have been working outside the home yourself. It would be worthwhile to write down exactly what and how much work you expect your husband to do, and then discuss your expectations with him. Work out a compromise that reflects your hope and his willingness to participate.

As you sit down and talk about delegating tasks, consider what each of your strengths are as parents. Your husband may be unsure what his strengths are as a father, so saying something like, "We have these children and we've got to be a team in raising them. What would you be willing to do, and what can I do?" may help reveal where his interests lie. If we use this approach, we're a lot more likely to give our husbands a chance to assert their gifts rather than trying to force them into some stereotype of what we think a father should do. For example, some women believe men should coach their son's soccer team. But that might be contrary to your husband's interests and abilities.

A Lesson from History

My husband learned more about the possibilities for his role as a father by studying some parenting models from the pages of history. Jonathan Edwards, for instance, set aside one hour each evening for his children. He and his wife would ask questions about their schooling and other subjects. With eleven children, Edwards' wife leaned heavily on him to participate. He was definitely the center point of the family.

—Gail

Knowing your strengths and weaknesses enables you and your husband to make the most of what you have to offer your children. Nobody's totally proficient at everything, nor do we all parent our children the same way. It says a lot about the stability of our relationship with our husband when we can tell a child, "You know, your father is better able to help you with that."

Likewise, allowing room for the differences in our parenting styles will help bring balance to our children's lives. For instance, the way a mother plays with her children is often drastically different from how her husband does. It's differences like these, though, that can help nurture the many facets of a growing child's personality.

Nurture a Thankful Heart

Perhaps the most important factor in getting our husbands more involved in parenting is to show genuine gratitude for the effort they do make in taking on more responsibility. When you see your husband make a move toward helping you, don't forget to show your appreciation. It might be tempting to say sarcastically, "Well, it's about time you helped me do this," or to be patronizing and say, "How wonderful—you tied Bobby's shoes!" But words like these will only sabotage your efforts to get him involved. A short acknowledgement of a helpful task is appropriate. And when somebody *sincerely* thanks me for doing something, I'm a lot more likely to want to do it again.

Your husband may not always live up to your expectations of the kind of father you want him to be to your children. But by showing him respect, approaching him positively, and thanking him for the job he does do with the kids, you're a lot more likely to see him become involved at home.

As the two of you become more of a parenting team, you can take advantage of the countless educational resources available. Read parenting magazines and books. Take in radio, television, and video programs, and attend seminars. Always be learners. With every stage of parenting comes new challenges. And once you learn to face them together, the team concept can enlarge to include the children. We can share each other's victories and defeats. We can offer support, instruction, and encouragement, each family member doing his part to help the others toward the goal—becoming more like Christ.

Making Room for Dad
Lin Grensing

There's a special bond that develops between mother and child. And sometimes that bond can make moms unaware of the equally important bond between father and child. How can moms learn to share the parenting responsibility? The following tips may help:

Share your feelings. Both mothers and fathers need not fear admitting to each other that they aren't "experts." The pregnancy and child-rearing experience conjures up all kinds of contradictory feelings—joy and fear, wonder and worry. Be open about all these emotions.

Become less self-centered. It's important for mothers to realize that husbands *are* involved. Parenting responsibilities can come between a couple if they become so tied up in the children that their own relationship suffers. Mothers are often surprised to realize that their hopes, fears, and concerns for their children are shared by their husbands.

Allow your husband to take the initiative. Parenting is a *shared* role. Mothers shouldn't see their task as *delegating* responsibilities to fathers. Fathers can take charge too. It's not unusual these days to find fathers with their children at doctors' offices, parent/teacher meetings, birthday parties—any number of traditionally "mother/child" outings.

Allow your husband to make mistakes. Let Dad spend time with the kids alone without watching to see that he's doing everything "right." Let him do parenting tasks his own way. Encourage him to be involved and give him positive feedback.

Keep talking. If there's any one thing Mom can do to "make room for Dad" it is to communicate, communicate, *communicate!* Talk often about the challenges and joys of parenting, and you'll find the bonds growing stronger between every member of the family.

From Today's Christian Woman
(May/June 1988)

Make It Happen

1. Often a man feels as though he's doing his part for the family just by going to work every day, especially if the wife is staying at home. Ask your husband to define his role in the family and see if being a breadwinner fills his expectation for the role he plays as father.

2. Ask your husband what child-rearing task he most enjoys. Allowing him to do what he considers to be fun will make it easier for him to be involved.

3. Sit down with your husband and come up with some times when you could have a break from the kids. See how he would feel about watching the children some Saturday without you. Point out the benefits of him having concentrated time with the kids. Maybe you could start with just a morning and work up to longer periods of time.

Chapter 16

HOW CAN I WIN OVER MY STEPCHILD?

Gail MacDonald

I f you're faced with the challenge of melding two sets of children from former marriages, it's only natural to gauge how well you're doing by whether or not your spouse's children have grown to accept and like you. While we'd like to believe we could form immediate and harmonious relationships within a new blended family, the reality of the situation is often quite different from the scenes portrayed on TV sitcoms. Winning over your children may be a legitimate goal, but it shouldn't be your immediate objective.

It's important to remember that for children living in a blended family, the rules have suddenly changed in the middle of the game. Having a stepmother was not the children's choice. And the loss of a mother, whether through divorce or death, has triggered a very necessary time of grief. You need to give children plenty of time and emotional breathing space to adjust to a new family.

The Stepmother Challenge

Studies have shown that stepmothers have greater difficulty integrating into the new family structure than stepfathers, especially when teenagers are involved. Not long ago, I read the book *All Grown Up and No Place to Go* by David Elkind. Of his study of 2,000 teenagers in Florida, a quarter of them from intact families reported significant stress at home. In the homes of teens living with a stepfather or a single parent, it rose to one-third. Yet fully half of the teenagers living with a stepmother reported a high level of stress in the home. Elkind further suggests that there are several reasons why stepmothers face a particularly difficult challenge.

First, you probably spend more time around your stepchildren than their father does, and that means more time for resentments to build. You're viewed as an intruder—someone who's taken over the place of the real mother.

Secondly, quite often stepmothers are younger than their husbands. If a teenaged stepchild is involved, the age gap between you and the children may simply be too small for realistic, effective discipline to take place. That creates a lot of pressure for you and the teenager.

Finally, many stepmothers may attempt to express affection too soon. Though it may come naturally for you, respect the children's feelings about affection. In particular, teenage stepchildren may feel extremely uncomfortable expressing affection toward you and receiving affection from you because they view it as disloyalty to their real mother.

A New Definition of Love

As you think about your role as a stepmother, it may help to refocus your goal. Rather than asking, "How do I want to love these children?" you might take an entirely different approach. Instead, try asking, "How do these children want to be loved?" Discovering the answer to that means understanding each child's needs, observing them, and entering into their world as they permit.

Be prepared to walk a fine line between taking an interest in your stepchildren and seeming nosey about their affairs. Kids know when you are being genuine and when they're being manipulated. It will take time for you to pick up the daily rhythms and family patterns these children are accustomed to.

It's easy to interpret a teenager's actions as rebellion and take it personally. Yet it may be the child acts a particular way by nature. For instance, if your stepson typically is quiet, he probably will turn inward even more under the stress of having his father remarry.

It Takes Time

As far as I know, there aren't any shortcuts when it comes to forming attachments with stepchildren. Judith Wallerstein, who directs the Center for the Family in Transition, says it takes anywhere from two to four years to form a new relationship, depending on how it is handled. It may help considerably if you work hard at being patient. Begin thinking in terms of years, not weeks or months, for adjustments to be made. That way, you can lower your expectations and you won't be so hard on yourself—or your stepchildren.

There's Only One

When you're a stepmother, you need to take care not to assume the role of stand-in for the real mother. The realities of the situation should be out in the open, and they should be discussed. You might want to speak very directly to your stepchildren, saying, "You only have one mother, and I'm not your mother. But I want to be your friend and stepmother."

Talk to your husband and ask him to make it clear to his children that it is a non-negotiable house rule that they respect you as an adult just as they are to respect any adult. They need to hear this from him.

—Kathy

Another factor to keep in mind with older children is the normal course of adolescent emotional development. A teenaged boy—regardless of the fact that he has a new stepmother—needs time and energy to develop his own identity apart from his parents. A lot of frustration is generated when he has to set aside the work of separating from his parents, and instead cope with a brand-new parent.

Along with patience, you need a great deal of sensitivity and openness about what is going on. Look for ways to defuse any sense of competition with the other mother, and instead, search for ways to affirm the good and unique things she did. Don't put the stepchildren in a defensive posture where they feel the need to prove their first mom was best.

Try asking a lot of questions, as a way of decoding your children's world. Preface your words in a way that lets your stepchildren know they can be open about their feelings. Reflect those feelings by saying things like, "I'm sure it's very difficult for you to see me in this role."

Another way to practice sensitivity involves how you speak to others about your new relationship. If you begin introducing your stepchild as "my son" or "my daughter" too quickly —before the children are ready— you may suffer more rejection. If the children bristle at being introduced that way, try to respect their feelings and not take it personally.

Call in the Support

Often stepchildren will project the hurt they feel about their situation onto their stepparent. While it might seem that the issue to be worked on is getting the children to accept you, the real objective is getting at the source of the children's woundedness. If they are acting out their pain toward you, you're in a tough situation. Thankfully, there are many resources today for handling stepparenting problems. Get all the help you can from friends in your church and community.

—Karen

Stepchildren also need to continue feeling as if their dad is on their team. That may mean being more discreet at home and in public with your displays of affection toward your husband. The children need reassurance that you won't rob them of their dad's affection. Stepchildren are likely to ask themselves, "How can Dad touch this woman the same way he touched Mom?" Look at stepparenting as a chance to "step into" the shoes of the child with whom you're attempting to build a relationship. The more you try to look at things from the child's point of view, the greater your chances of moving cautiously and carefully into a rewarding parenting experience.

Undoubtedly, this whole process will feel overwhelming

and frustrating at times. Remember that God can fill you with his divine, unconquerable love. You may not be able to change your stepchildren, but you can control the way you treat them and respond to them. With God's guidance, you can demonstrate grace and patience toward them.

You're Not My Real Mom
Jay Kessler

Blending together two distinct families under one roof isn't as simple as it appears. In fact, it can be terribly stressful to any marriage. Add the pain and grief your children may feel from the loss of a parent through death or divorce to their insecurity about this new relationship, and the potential for emotional fall-out is great. But there is light at the end of the tunnel for any Christian parent facing this delicate challenge.

Daring to Discipline

"I thought I would die when Michael's daughter screamed at me, 'You're not my real mom—get off my case!' after I tried to discipline her."

For this woman and others, discipline can be a sticky issue. Many times with divorce, children develop behavior problems that need to be addressed—but who is the one to do it? Except for very young children, discipline still should be the biological parent's duty. In difficult situations, bringing in a third party—such as a counselor or pastor—can be extremely helpful.

In the end, most blended families find discipline is best handled with a more participatory approach—a negotiated relationship. If anything, children in a blended family probably need to be asked about their opinions on certain issues more often. One good way to encourage open communication is to schedule a weekly family council night so each person can provide his input on what realistic guidelines and expectations for your new family should be.

Detective Work

If your child or stepchild acts angry or withdrawn, it's important to get to the source of the problem. Your child may know he's feeling depressed, but may not be able to put his finger on the specific reason. However, behavior problems such as flunking grades, breaking a curfew, or emotional blowups can stem from insecurity. Have your kids been uprooted to a new school and neighborhood? Do your stepchildren miss their other parent? They may resent the intrusive changes in their lives. Sometimes, however, a child may simply be testing you. He subconsciously thinks, *If this person puts up with me, she must really like me after all.* Be alert to the clues that point to the real reason your child acts up.

Peace with the Past

Chances are, you're caught up in the joy and healing your new marriage relationship brings. But unfortunately, these feelings don't automatically transfer to your kids. Hopefully, you and your spouse have buried the past—but remember, your kids may not have. Even after microscopic surgery, a scar remains. As Christian parents, we long for the pain a failed relationship or death inflicts on our children to disappear without a trace. But it doesn't.

However, the first step toward healing comes with accepting the responsibility for the hurt we've caused—and that's where the power of the gospel comes into play. The hope of redemption is that good can be brought out of difficult situations, but the elements of redemption—confession and repentance—are crucial. If your situation stems from a divorce, make sure you tell your children, "I'm sorry for the pain I've caused. I need your help to rebuild. Will you help me?"

Centuries ago the apostle Paul wrote, "But one thing I do: Forgetting what is behind and straining toward what is ahead, I press on . . ." (Philippians 3:14). Blended families can press forward, too. While creating one new family out of two can be incredibly tough, it can be done. With maturity, effort, and patience, you *can* rebuild—with God's help.

Adapted from Today's Christian Woman
(September/October 1991)

Make It Happen

1. Keep a healthy perspective toward your other relationships. Don't allow this problem area to dominate your marriage.

2. Give yourself and your stepchildren time. Remember, it could take years to establish a good relationship.

3. Encourage the relationship between your husband and his children. Suggest activities or create opportunities for concentrated one-on-one time.

4. Pray. Ask God for his continual wisdom and patience in working through your situation. Remember, he is with you every step of the way.

Chapter 17

HOW CAN I MAKE UP FOR THE SHORTCOMINGS OF A SINGLE-PARENT HOME?
Gail MacDonald

There's no question in my mind, single parents face some of the greatest challenges in parenting today—especially in our society where the support of an extended family is often lacking. Single mothers carry an enormous burden. So if you're trying to do the job of two parents, it's not surprising that you sometimes focus on the possible shortcomings of your situation rather than the positive, capable job you are doing.

Beware of this trap. If you resent your situation, even subconsciously, it can create anxiety in your children. They may feel they're a burden, or that the situation is their fault. Any resentment needs to be acknowledged before you can successfully do the work of two parents. And children will always be better off with a parent who accepts rather than fights against what life has dealt.

I have a single friend who has every reason to gripe about her situation, yet she doesn't. Instead she has chosen not to make single parenting the focus of her life. It's just a fact, and she handles it like any other life occurrence. This attitude frees her to be a good parent.

I noticed this in the way she often touches and affirms her children. It's obvious she delights in being around them. Letting children know they're loved and valued, and not a burden, is crucial for any parent. But single parents may have to make a special effort to communicate these things because in the press of daily life they can easily get squeezed out.

Taking a Guilt Trip

Besides resentment, another common trap for single mothers is to feel guilty for the things she can't provide, whether the situation is objectively her fault or not. But guilt only makes us ineffective as parents, deterring us from setting necessary limits for our children. And youngsters in single-parent homes need the same consistency and discipline as children in other homes. As a single mom, though, you'll have to work a little harder to maintain consistency because you don't have the support of a spouse with whom you can share the job of disciplining.

Here's where a support group may prove a life-saver. I know that time is a very real issue for any single parent, but you may find that the benefits of attending a single-parent support group are well worth the time you invest. Being a single parent is extremely stressful, and stress tends to make you put your own needs above the needs of the children. You switch to "survival mode," and it's all too easy to hurry the children into taking on too much responsibility too soon.

It's dangerous, for instance, to encourage the son to be "the man of the house." Or to make a child your confidant—asking her permission for you to date, or talking over matters that are only appropriate for adult ears. Get your adult needs met by adults, and you'll be better able to be the adult parent your children need.

——— ⚬⚭⚬ ———

Nurturing healthy relationships with other adults not only helps you, it helps your children. Don't limit yourself only to other single parents; surround yourself and your family with other families, or even with older students who can be positive role models. You may have to take the initiative, at least in the beginning, but don't hesitate to do so. Keep it simple and casual: "The children and I are going to fix a main dish; would you bring salad and dessert?" By regularly inviting people into your home, you are creating the possibility for solid relationships to form between your children and other adults and families.

Seeing your children interact with others—both adults and their own peers—gives you important feedback on how they're doing. Other children will draw out your children in a way adults can't. Other adults will provide potential role models and examples of different ways of doing things. Again, all children need these things, but especially those in single-family homes. You can be looking for families in which a healthy marriage is modeled and for men who can provide the kind of nurturing your children need.

Besides informal relationships that can develop as you provide these kinds of opportunities, there are formal programs you can look into. Many churches and communities have "Big Brother/Little Brother" programs, where an adult male is matched up with a young boy to make up for the lack of a father. Another program to look into is "Adopt a Grandparent," in which a single-parent child develops a special relationship with a loving senior.

Don't Raise Spies

If your ex-husband spends time with your children regularly, resist the temptation to make your children into "spies." Don't ask for a report on who their father may be spending time with. This turns your children into tattletales and asks them to be disloyal to their father.

On the other hand, be interested in what they see and experience when they are with their dad, and talk about it naturally without prying. This is especially important if your ex-husband has some questionable behaviors—such as drinking—that you want to discuss with your children.

—Karen

No one can replace a father, but God can use loving men to provide the guidance and nurturing needed from a man. A special relationship with a neighbor, a friend, a grandfather, a teacher, or coach can go a long way in supplying that need.

Take Time to Heal

Before your children can be truly open to surrogate father relationships, however, they need to work through their grief over the relationship they lost with their real father. They need to be able to talk about their feelings. Someone once said, "We heal our wounds by talking about them." Allow your children to express their emotions. Help your children learn to be honest about their feelings by being appropriately open about your own. It's okay, even good, to let them see that you hurt sometimes, too. But discuss your strongest feelings with adults only. Your children also need your strength.

Be honest, too, about the limits of your resources—time, money, material goods. Here again, you're the one who sets the tone. Be matter-of-fact and positive, instead of expressing self-pity. "There's a limit to our finances, and this is why you can't have designer clothes. But you can choose your own clothes within our budget. And let's all work at being thankful that we do have enough." If you struggle with the changes, admit it. But then try to move on to the positive. In this way you will demonstrate how to deal with grief and get on with life.

Remember God's Unique Promises

Although you may be struggling with the pressures of being a single mother, don't underestimate what you *can* do for your children. Yes, there may be some deficiencies in your home because your children don't have their father around. But God has promised to take special care of widows and fatherless children. Pray that he will provide loving, strong men who will take an interest in your children and become healthy role models. Surround yourself with other families, so that your children can observe and absorb how healthy marriages work. But realize that you have a crucial role to play, and that, as you do your best, their heavenly Father can make up for the lacks in your children's lives.

—◆—

John Trent, co-author of *The Blessing* and *The Language of Love*, came from a single-parent home. His mother had determined that her sons would learn to love their heavenly Father through her own consistent loving care of them. John comments that she was successful because she committed herself to them and showed them love through what he calls "contact and caring points."

The first contact and caring point was when she got them up in the morning. She consistently tried to communicate a sense that "this is going to be a good day." And when she dropped them off for school, she let them know they would be enveloped in her prayers and that they could get through anything today with the love of Jesus. And she would try to be home when the children came home, to provide the opportunity for them to share their day. Eating dinner together was mandatory—a time to affirm their togetherness. Finally, the last words at night for them when they went to bed was that their mom was there for them, and always would be. John says he thinks she worked hard to live out Proverbs 15:30: "Bright eyes gladden the heart, and good news puts fat on the bones" (NASB).

His mother's eyes would brighten when she was with her children, showing how much she enjoyed each of them as people. Her consistent upbeat attitude and cheerful words did much to build a solid foundation for him and his brothers.

———※———

Trent also talks about the importance of teamwork in his family. As they all contributed to making the home run smoothly, they felt responsible, needed, and bonded to each other. The boys knew Mom couldn't do it without them. Yet their mother never tried to make any of the boys the head of the home. She just helped them realize that each member was a necessary part of the whole. Healthy responsibility is both balanced—everyone pitches in—and geared toward the age level of the child.

Trent's mother let her children know that she was doing the best she could to be both father and mother with the strength God gave her—and trusting him to fill in the gaps. In the end that's what each of us must do, single parent or not: do the best we can, and trust God to make up for our imperfections. Because he is faithful, we can believe that he will do it.

A Checklist for Single Parents
Denise Turner

Today millions of single adults are working double time to raise a family and bring home a salary. If you happen to be one of those parents, you know how difficult it can be to balance your various responsibilities. To help you cope, answer the following questions:

• Have I accepted that very small children cannot fully understand either the divorce or the death of a parent? Am I patient with them, explaining the situation to them in simple terms? Have I prepared myself to deal with their needs and feelings and periods of self-blame?

• Do I know that children whose parents have divorced must experience a grieving process similar to that of children who have lost a parent through death? Am I prepared to deal with denial, shock, anger, and all kinds of feelings and reactions?

• Have I found a way to reassure my children that I will never stop loving them, even if the bond of love between me and their father has been broken?

• Do I allow my children privacy and silence when they need it—and do I encourage them to talk when they need to?

• Have I requested a conference with my children's teachers so that they can work with me in helping my children to cope?

• Do I work hard to consider my children's needs when planning visitations? Do I make sure I never give my children the impression that they must choose sides?

• Do I catch myself when tempted to demand too much of myself? Do I fight any feelings of guilt? Do I refrain from blaming everything bad that happens in my family on the absence of a father figure?

• Do I make a real effort to have a life of my own apart from my children, so that I will not place on them the extra burden of filling my needs?

• Is the key focus in my life built around love—of self, of others, and of God?

From Today's Christian Woman
(May/June 1988)

Make It Happen

1. Analyze your parenting skills. What are the best things you have to offer your children? Do you know how to have fun? Are you a good conversationalist? Make the most of these qualities and spend less time fretting over your weaknesses.

2. Pick out families in your church you admire and invite them over for a day. Have simple meals together and play family games. These informal times with two-parent families can help build friendships between your children and adult men. That way, when your children need a man to talk to, and their father

isn't available, they'll have someone in place.

3. Free yourself from the guilt trap. Have a phrase you repeat in your mind whenever guilt sneaks up on you. Say something like, "I'm giving my children the best upbringing I can. I have nothing to feel bad about."

Chapter 18

HOW CAN I GET MY CHILDREN TO BECOME FRIENDS WITH EACH OTHER?
Kathy Peel

I admire a mother's desire for her children to become friends with each other. After all, one of the greatest rewards of having kids is watching them learn to love one another and grow together as a family. But not all brothers and sisters have personalities that would naturally draw them to each other. Rather than push our children to be friends, I feel it's more important that we strive to develop mutual respect and the ability to enjoy each other's company.

Part of learning to live in a family is learning how to deal with the little things that bother us. Hopefully, this prepares our children to live peacefully with future roommates and, ultimately, a spouse. I'm convinced that one of the primary reasons kids bicker and don't get along is because they get bored. Mom and Dad are too busy, too tired, or too stressed out to spend time exclusively with the family.

———— ❧ ————

One of the best ways to begin fostering mutual respect and enjoyment of each other is to orchestrate fun family activities and outings. Go fishing and help each other reel in the catch. Plan a

135

picnic or a visit to a local museum. Ask your children for ideas.

One thing I endorse is long car trips for vacation. While most parents dread the thought of spending several hours in the car with the kids, I found that all it takes to turn it into a positive experience is a little bit of planning. For instance, have systems set up for who chooses the cassette tape and whose turn it is to sit by the window. This way you eliminate a lot of the things they would normally quarrel about. Plan fun activities for the car ride ahead of time so you're prepared when the kids start feeling antsy.

Am I the Cause?

One of the things I did when the children were fighting was examine how I might be contributing to the problem. Very often sibling rivalry indicated to me that one of the children was not feeling justly attended to. So I would take a good look at whether I was playing favorites or giving that compliant middle child enough of me.

I also learned that kids who bicker and don't get along very well when they are young, often grow up to become the best of friends. My two sons are a classic example. They used to drive me crazy with their bickering, but now they are great buddies. Sometimes we just need to give our children time. Often they'll become friends when they've grown up.

—Karen

Give a Little Space

On the other hand, don't make your children do everything together. I don't like the idea of making little brother tag along. That can make siblings resent each other. Sometimes I've gotten a babysitter for the youngest one rather than take him on an outing with the older kids. It would have been cheaper to take him along, but the older boys needed their space.

It's good to talk about giving each other space and respecting each others' feelings. We have faced this with our two older boys. Our seventeen-year-old and thirteen-year-old share a bedroom that isn't very big. One of the boys is somewhat messy, and the other one is neat and orderly. Every once in a while we have to take them aside and say, "Okay, John, you need to be sensitive to Joel's need for order. And Joel, you need to be sensitive to John's need to be creative. Let's work it out." Everybody has to give a little, respecting each other's unique design.

We're trying to help our children learn how to work through conflict. We'll sit them down on the sofa and hear both sides of the story, talk it through, and see where the bottom line is. Sometimes problems can feel like a ball of twine; it's all gnarled up and you have to pull the right string to get it straightened out.

I don't expect my children to be perfect. I know the older ones get impatient with their six-year-old brother, who happens to be quite verbose. Yet I do expect all of us to be kind to each other, saying in a nice way, "James, would you please be quiet. I'm trying to do something," instead of, "James, shut up!"

I admit to having a very low tolerance for harsh words. We are all worthwhile, uniquely made individuals, worthy of each other's respect. Consequently, I come down hard on kids who talk ugly to each other. To help my children get a handle on these all-too-common verbal assaults, I try to set the example for them. I've even told them, "If you ever hear Dad and me talking unkindly, then you can do it." It's not right for me to say "don't talk ugly" if I talk rudely to my husband or my child. You have to practice what you preach. If you're willing to set the example, then I feel you have the freedom to say, "We don't talk like that at our house. We do not cut people down."

Are You Building?

Once, when our children were about five and eight, they were caught arguing. I can remember my husband stopping them and saying, "This is home. Now, outside of these four walls people are going to hurt you, they're going to call you names. But inside these four walls we build each other. Do you understand? We build each other."

And that became a by-word in our home. Are you building? Many times when Gordon or I would say something derogatory to each other, the children would say, "Mother, was that a building comment?" When everybody gets on the building bandwagon, it makes a big difference.

—Gail

Family Ties

We have a saying in our house, and I believe it's true: "To belittle is to be little." You're just being a small person if you find it necessary to cut someone else down. One principle we try to instill into our children's lives is that we're a family and we stick up for each other. If somebody's cutting another family member down, we stick up for each other.

Although it is my desire to see our children form solid friendships with each other, the most important thing to me is that they learn to love each other unconditionally and work together as a family. If we can accomplish that, they will be far better equipped to go out into the world and begin their own families.

Understanding Sibling Rivalry
Jay Kesler

Most of us are quick to label any form of bickering between our children as sibling rivalry. But before we make this assumption, we must first understand what sibling rivalry is—and what it isn't.

First, it helps to understand that the psychologists who coined the expression "sibling rivalry" did so with the underlying presupposition that children are innocent at birth and later corrupted by society. As Christians, however, we accept the biblical belief that humans are born in sin. Whether we like it or not, our children are born selfish, envious, greedy, and jealous.

So it really shouldn't come as a surprise when we see sibling rivalry. Name calling and fighting merely are the acting out of inherent traits in our children.

While we may accept modern psychological terms, it's important not to automatically accept the assumptions behind them. When we do that, we build ourselves up for more parenting stress than is necessary.

As parents there are a number of things we can do to bring peace and tranquility to a house where sibling rivalry is an ongoing problem. To begin with, remember that your primary task as a Christian parent is to move your child toward a relationship with Christ. As you do, self-centeredness—the real cause of sibling tensions—slowly diminishes.

Positive sibling relationships begin with parents who model fairness. Treat each of your children with respect and concern, based on your child's particular circumstances, needs, and personality.

As a parent who enters the room after an argument has begun, you're at a disadvantage. But you can still model fairness by saying, "The television goes off until both of you can come to a compromise without fighting." Surprisingly, when one child isn't declared the winner and both lose out on a privilege, they can usually work something out. Besides modeling fairness, you're also encouraging your children to resolve their own conflicts.

Be patient as you try to help your children understand the concept of fairness. It's helpful to remember it will take many explanations and actions for fairness to replace selfishness.

Next, it helps to look at what expectations you are setting for your family. Although it takes more time, our children need more than a reprimand—they need a reason why the behavior isn't acceptable. It's much better to say, "Don't hit your sister, because in this family we love each other. It makes me sad when you hit someone I love."

Words can also set the tone for positive sibling relations. One family I know has a rule that the words "shut up" directed toward any family member would not be tolerated. Such words were considered a put-down and devalued a family member. When statements like this are kept to a minimum, a sense of respect develops as does an atmosphere of love.

When we see our children bickering and fighting, we sometimes assume they don't like each other. In reality, that is very seldom the case. Our children are learning to share and to be fair. And to master these skills, they work them out with those closest to them—brothers and sisters. So when we view sibling rivalry as an expected part of growing up, it helps us set reasonable expectations for ourselves and our children.

Adapted from Today's Christian Woman
(March/April 1991)

Make It Happen

1. If you haven't done this already, sit down with your children and review some guidelines on how they are to treat each other. What kind of language is allowed? How are they to "make up" after an argument?

2. Help your children learn to affirm each other. Help one make a card or a poster for another. Encourage them to pray for each other. Help them verbalize what they like about each other.

Chapter 19

HOW DO I BECOME FRIENDS WITH MY ADULT CHILDREN?

Karen Mains

A mother in my church related a story about her daughter who attended her twenty-year high school reunion. The daughter's friends were complaining about their mothers: "Mine calls me every day to tell me what's wrcng with my life," one said. "My mother feels as though she has to approve of everything I do," said another. Then my friend's daughter spoke up. "My mother is not that way. She doesn't try to control me or run my life. She's there when I need her—she's my friend."

Would that all mothers earned such praise. For me, my relationships with my adult children have evolved into a mixture of mother and friend. I'll admit it's been a learning process, working out this dynamic of becoming mother/friend rather than just parent/child. I'm still freeing them, affirming them, and giving them permission to grow. And they're still trying to get my ear. I'm a friend, but I truly am Mother, and always will be. What I'm beginning to realize is that this shift in our relationship is a process—one that needs regular evaluation both on my part and theirs.

Building Mutual Expectations

This may sound odd, but the only way to begin establishing an adult friendship with your children is to describe your desires for an adult relationship with them and find out what their expectations are, too. We can't just assume we know. Adult children need to define what they expect and need from their parents. For instance, I asked my children simple yet vital questions like, "Do you want me to call you every week? Do you want to know about my travel plans? Would you welcome a standing invitation to Sunday dinner?"

Some adult children are resistant to on-going family relationships. If this is the case, it might help to ask your children to define what they want out of the family, and then begin a negotiation process. Try to find a median between what the adult children want and what you want. And then try to get them to open up about why they feel the way they do.

As children become adults and establish their own lives, holidays inevitably can become a major dilemma. You might expect them home, yet they have plans to ski the Rockies. I avoided the holiday hassle by releasing control. While it wasn't easy at first, I allowed my kids the freedom to negotiate their own holiday schedules. I didn't expect them to spend every Christmas with us. And once the sense of freedom was established, I found my kids more open to joining family gatherings.

I remember one Thanksgiving they all decided to join us at a retreat house someone had loaned us. I organized the weekend, with everyone taking charge of a meal and an evening's activities. We had plenty of time for sharing, games, and horseback riding. It was a wonderful time with lots of laughter. I admit, I wish we could be together as a family like that for every holiday. But I try to keep in mind that there are many other times of the year to spend together that aren't as stress-filled as the holidays.

———⚬❦⚬———

My adult children have told me they'd like me to be more involved in their lives. I would much rather have them complain about me being under-involved than being over-involved. Establishing the right level of involvement is critical to good relationships with our adult children. If you sense your children resent your involvement, back off. Let them call the shots.

This can be a threatening prospect, especially if you've built your life around your kids. Part of the tension of building an adult-level friendship with our children is recognizing that they may have outgrown us. Many children end up being more educated than their mothers, and the mothers may feel intimidated by their children's maturity or intellectual prowess. If you feel your children are passing you by, try to realize what this means for you as their mother. Isn't this what we want for our children— what is the best for *them*? I strongly believe that when our children surpass our level of education or ability in certain areas, it marks a significant feat in our mission as mothers. We can happily shout,"Hurrah, this is wonderful."

Adult Siblings as Friends

Beyond my own interest in becoming a friend to my adult children, it's also important to me that my kids learn how to relate to one another as adults. I think the support and nurturing that comes out of sibling relationships is critical for the future of a family. I would want to know that if something were to happen to me or my husband, our children could find their way to one another.

I think that's one of the rules for parenting adults: encourage and give permission for sibling relationships to form. Some

Do They Really Need Me?

As much as I would love to live in the same town as our adult children, I am honestly aware that, at least for this period in their married lives, it's good that I am at a distance. I am a consummate nurturer who loves to give and help, even if that help isn't what's best. I'm forever asking myself if help is what is needed and if they truly desire this from me.

Keeping that question in the forefront of my thinking has given me balance and added to two very fulfilling relationships with our married daughter and daughter-in-law. But I need to keep asking myself these questions lest I become insensitive and do lasting harm to what are two beautiful relationships.
—Gail

parents feel nervous about this. They're afraid their kids will talk about Mom and Dad. And they probably will. I'm glad our children have one another to complain to.

Our children appear to be very close, but their relationships still need to be encouraged. One practical way I've been able to reach this goal is by not allowing the children to gripe to me about one another. I encourage them to settle their differences with each other, just as I need to settle any tensions I may feel between me and my children.

The Job That Never Ends

I don't think we ever quit parenting. And hopefully our children will still be learning from us when we're seventy-five. I met a seventy-five-year-old woman at a retreat recently, and I thought, I want to be like her. She has given her life to helping her children and her grandchildren learn. She takes them on educational trips and sends them books. And she keeps learning herself. In fact, she learned to sail when she was seventy-two!

—Kathy

Forgiving the Past

For instance, we've had some frank discussions with our young adult children where they have told us how it hurt them that we were not available for them as much as they would have liked us to be. Often if an adult child does pull away, it is in response to some hurts they experienced in their childhood.

All of our kids have had to confront us about things that were hurtful to them. But all along I've said to them, "I'm not a perfect parent and I will probably do things I don't mean to do."

Ever since they were little, when I would lose my temper, I would say to them, "I blew it and I need you to forgive Mommy." So it's not hard for me to do that now. If you've never asked your children's forgiveness, it's a little more frightening. But it's part of the process of becoming righteous. It's worthwhile to find a way to humble oneself and seek forgiveness.

It's hard to open up about past hurts. Unfortunately, even if a parent says, "Tell me how I've hurt you," that doesn't mean that parent is willing to hear, and the adult children may sense that. Sometimes family counseling is in order. You might consider reading a book together on those hurtful areas and discussing it.

The popular books on co-dependency might be good starters. Better to resolve issues as adults than to go on living with hurt and resentment.

Once a Parent, Always a Parent

While becoming friends with our adult children is a wonderful reward for years of doing the hard work of parenting, we have to remember that in the end we are still their parents. Our relationship will continue to grow and evolve over the years. Inevitably, we will see ourselves slipping back into a parental mode—especially if we see our adult children making choices we strongly disagree with. So we need to be patient with the process and realize that the shift from a parent/child to adult/child relationship is a gradual one. But it's one worth pursuing as your children's needs for you as a mother change.

Make It Happen

1. Casually ask your adult children if your level of involvement in their lives is appropriate. Make adjustments according to their response.

2. Remember, you can only change yourself. For instance, if your adult children pull away from the family for a time, work on your own attitude rather than trying to change your children.

3. While your mothering role has changed, it hasn't ended. Be sure you're still giving your children affirmation and support, even though they're "all grown up."

4. Discuss holiday plans months in advance. Try to give up your expectations and allow your adult children to decide what they want to do. Your children will deeply appreciate you not pressuring them, and it may make them more likely to choose to be with you.

Epilogue

AN ANCHOR IN
A CRAZY WORLD

T he 1990s may well be the toughest decade yet to raise children. But what gives a Christian parent the edge, as Gail, Karen, and Kathy continually pointed out, is that we don't go it alone. God is with us every step of the way—for strength, guidance, and hope. What an assurance to cling to as we prepare our children for what seems like a "crazy" world—one full of pressures *our* parents never even imagined.

As we go about the business of raising our children, several common threads run through the insights shared in this book.

First and foremost, we must make the time, take the time, to *listen*—beginning when our children speak their first words. Listening, as Karen notes, is the foundation to so many essentials in raising kids—like self-esteem and self-respect.

Second, we must *nurture uniqueness*. As Kathy said so well, it begins by seeing ourselves as a farmer, not an architect who builds something new. We must take what is inherent in the seed and cultivate it in a good environment.

Finally, we must continually *look to the Lord*—our heavenly Father. When we keep our focus on him and remember the compassion, patience, and unconditional love he has for us, we can then be encouraged and strengthened to face the daily challenges we have as parents.

Today's Christian Woman is a positive, practical magazine designed for contemporary Christian women of all ages, single or married, who seek to live out biblical values in their homes, workplaces, and communities. With honesty and warmth, *Today's Christian Woman* provides depth, balance, and perspective to the issues that confront women today.

If you would like a subscription to *Today's Christian Woman* send your name and address to *Today's Christian Woman*, P.O. Box 11618, Des Moines, Iowa 50340. Subscription rates: one year (6 issues) $14.95, or two years (12 issues) $23.60.